PRAISE FOR *THE GREAT*
TO MAKE PUBLIC EDU~~~~ ~~~ ~~ORK IN AMERICA

"Want challenging, inspiring, and supportive schools? Read *The Great Equalizer: Six Strategies to Make Public Education Work in America* to learn how it was done in Meriden, Connecticut. This beautiful, inspiring, and practical book packed with key takeaways and guiding questions illustrates the importance of laying the foundation for innovation with stakeholder partnerships and celebrating progress on a dashboard of success. Learn how to embrace whole child design principles in a tech-enabled learning environment where all students are challenged and supported."

—**Tom Vander Ark,** CEO, Getting Smart; former executive
director, Education, Bill and Melinda Gates Foundation;
author, *Smart Cities That Work for Everyone*

"Today's modern learners deserve an experience that is relevant for the world in which they live and will work. Shifting paradigms and systems is not easy. It requires bold decision-making, visionary leadership, and resilience to get the work done. Yet, *it is possible.* There is no better way to make the necessary shifts happen than to learn from those leading the work, and this book highlights what's happening in Meriden Public Schools, one of the best district turnaround stories in the country. *The Great Equalizer* provides an evidence-based, experientially grounded framework for educational leaders to effectively reimagine what's possible while developing a course of action to make it happen. No matter where you find the state of your system today, this book will force reflection while guiding you in leading the work to new heights."

—**Thomas C. Murray,** Director of Innovation, Future Ready Schools,
Washington, DC; best-selling author of *Personal and Authentic:
Designing Learning Experiences That Impact a Lifetime* and *Learning
Transformed: 8 Keys to Designing Tomorrow's Schools, Today*

"The voices of practitioners are all too often left out of the conversation about what we need to do to transform our schools and systems. But if we want to serve all students better in our public schools, we need to understand the stories and perspectives of the leaders who have actually done the work. Mark D. Benigni, Barbara A. Haeffner, and Lois B. Lehman offer solid guidance based on their real experiences successfully improving adult practice and student outcomes. The six strategies they recommend can be applied in any system and will lead to better learning for all students."

—**Joshua P. Starr EdD,** CEO of PDK International, former
superintendent of the Montgomery County Public Schools

"*The Great Equalizer: Six Strategies to Make Public Education Work in America* is an important resource for leaders to reiterate that indeed, public education in America remains the great equalizer for our students and families. The six strategies all center around embracing, teaching, and nurturing the Whole Child. Now, more than ever before, educators need to be reminded of the importance of engaging the community to reach and support every learner."

> **—Valerie Truesdale PhD,** assistant executive director, AASA,
> the Superintendents Association; former Chief Transformation and
> Technology Officer for Charlotte-Mecklenburg Schools, NC

"Under Mark D. Benigni's leadership, Meriden Public Schools has been a national lighthouse for exemplary school system leadership and has been honored for its innovation with technology. It is impressive how they work as a team with their community to build equitable digital learning environments while embracing social-emotional wellbeing and ensuring student-centered learning. Learn these impressive lessons for all school leaders and those who want a better education for our children."

> **—Keith Krueger,** CEO, Consortium for School Networking (CoSN)

"One great lesson learned during the recent past is that 'leadership matters!' Effective collaboration is the secret sauce behind the success of most leadership endeavors. Connecticut's Meriden Public Schools district leaders, who authored this book, exemplify the epitome of collaborative leadership on a daily basis. Readers of *The Great Equalizer: Six Strategies to Make Public Education Work in America* will come away with winning strategies and immediate and long-term action steps to ensure that their schools are truly meeting the current and future needs of all their students."

> **—Ann McMullan,** National Education Leadership Consultant

"*The Great Equalizer* is an essential book at a critical time. With intelligent analysis and compelling storytelling, the authors have taken us inside the work of Meriden Public Schools. It is time that policymakers, researchers, and practitioners all know about Meriden's focused, innovative, and sustained improvement efforts. Theirs is the story of what matters most: doing whatever is possible to ensure that each and every child experiences educational success."

> **—Richard W. Lemons,** executive director,
> Partners for Educational Leadership

"Of all the districts we have worked with, Meriden Public Schools operates administratively with enthusiasm. There is no resting on their laurels there, but a tone of constant innovation. Their digital transition supports students with heightened humanity—a real trick to pull off in schools that takes a changed mindset. Therefore, superintendent Benigni and his superb staff were awarded the Learning Counsel News Media & Research's high honor of 'EduJedi Knighthood,' one of only four districts nationwide to make it to that level in 2020. As an author myself, I am pleased to endorse their book *The Great Equalizer: Six Strategies to Make Public Education Work in America.*"

—**LeiLani Cauthen,** CEO and publisher, The Learning
Counsel; author, *The Consumerization of Learning*

"We are in the midst of a STEM workforce shortage. Countries around the world are gearing up to fill these jobs from where they sit. Dr. Benigni and his team are doing the work that prepares students to thrive, not just survive, in the rest of the 21st century. *The Great Equalizer: Six Strategies to Make Public Education Work in America* is a blueprint for the post-pandemic development of our young people to compete globally."

—**Marlon Lindsay,** founder and CEO of 21stCentEd; coauthor of
STEM Century: It Takes a Village to Raise a 21st Century Graduate

"Having worked for many years with the leadership at Meriden schools, I have seen how their consistency, high standards, and understanding of their students and community pay off for every student. I highly recommend *The Great Equalizer* for every school district.*"

—**Larry Jacobs,** president and publisher, American Consortium
for Equity in Education; host of "Education Talk Radio"

The Great Equalizer

Clayton,
Thank you
for being a champion
for public education!

Mark
Barnepin

The Great Equalizer

Six Strategies to Make Public Education Work in America

Mark D. Benigni
Barbara A. Haeffner
Lois B. Lehman

ROWMAN & LITTLEFIELD
Lanham • Boulder • New York • London

Published by Rowman & Littlefield
An imprint of The Rowman & Littlefield Publishing Group, Inc.
4501 Forbes Boulevard, Suite 200, Lanham, Maryland 20706
www.rowman.com

86-90 Paul Street, London EC2A 4NE, United Kingdom

British Library Cataloguing in Publication Information Available

Library of Congress Cataloging-in-Publication Data

Names: Benigni, Mark D., 1971– author. | Haeffner, Barbara A., 1966– author. | Lehman, Lois B., 1934– author.
Title: The great equalizer : six strategies to make public education work in America / Mark D. Benigni, Barbara A. Haeffner, Lois B. Lehman.
Description: Lanham : Rowman & Littlefield Publishing Group, [2022] | Includes index. | Summary: "The Great Equalizer: Six Strategies to Make Public Education Work in America shares six strategies to ensure that American public education remains the Great Equalizer by addressing how to solve growing inequalities and increasing student needs. Chapter takeaways and discussion questions offer a glimpse into the reality of leading public education"—Provided by publisher.
Identifiers: LCCN 2021051880 (print) | LCCN 2021051881 (ebook) | ISBN 9781475864090 (cloth) | ISBN 9781475864106 (paperback) | ISBN 9781475864113 (epub)
Subjects: LCSH: Educational equalization—United States. | Public schools—Social aspects—United States. | Education—Aims and objectives—United States.
Classification: LCC LC213.2 .B46 2022 (print) | LCC LC213.2 (ebook) | DDC 379.2/60973—dc23/eng/20220217
LC record available at https://lccn.loc.gov/2021051880
LC ebook record available at https://lccn.loc.gov/2021051881

To the Meriden Public School's students, staff, and families

Contents

Preface

Everyone needs an advocate, and I was one of the lucky ones to have total support from my family. I experienced this early in my schooling. I still remember matching two boats and pronouncing the word boats, already excited and ready to locate the airplane and the car. I was in first grade and working with a speech pathologist. As a former student with speech and language difficulties and having spent seven years teaching special education students in a public school setting, I know firsthand the importance of providing all students with the support they need.

I was beginning my eighth grade year at my neighborhood public middle school, and my dad once again went to bat for me. See, my dad was honest and hard-working—in love with the same woman his entire life—and determined to provide a better life for his three sons. I guess, in so many ways, I was the lucky one! He was my dad. He was my advocate. So, where do I begin?

In the mid-1960s, this small urban community, known as the Silver City, was a place where factory jobs were plentiful, and getting ahead in life was still possible through hard work, with or without an education.

My mom and dad married young. My mom was 19, and my dad was just 18. My parents came from very humble beginnings. They had nothing but a love for each other and a dream for their family. I had two parents, who were my advocates, and they knew education was my brothers' and my only chance for a better life. Although not college-educated themselves, my parents were adamant that their children would go to college, and they were not afraid to come into school and advocate for us.

But today, I am seeing many children from all different circumstances left to navigate the system without any help. How can we make sure public education works for them? How can we help them define their destiny? So this brings me back to my eighth grade year. As I attended my morning classes on the first day of school, I was glad to see friends and excited about the start of the new school year. After lunch, my day took a turn for the worst, but my life took a turn for the better. I still wonder if this day was when my future was sealed and my destiny was defined. This day would guide my leadership through high school, college, and my career in education.

It was math period and, while all my friends were heading to Algebra 1, I was heading to Grade 8 Math. How could this be? I knew I always got straight As, and I thought I was pretty good at math. I could not hold it together, so I went to the office and did what any teenage boy would do when he was upset. Yes, I called my mom, who called my dad, who proceeded to leave work and come to school.

My dad never missed work. I am not even sure he got paid if he did. He worked in a local factory. As I waited in the office, the principal told me my dad was on his way, and I became even more upset. Would he be mad at me? Would he think I was a baby? Would he lose his job? And why was I so upset? Should I just sit through my math class and get another A? So I sat shaking on the bench in the main office and waited for my father.

I knew I had to pull it together and clearly explain to my dad why this mattered so much to me. While he would not know the difference between Algebra 1 and Grade 8 Math, he would know that you do not set limits on children, especially his, and no one blocks his kids from reaching their goals and creating their best futures. As my dad entered the school, I felt an uplifting spirit, and I was so glad to see him. I knew he would advocate for me, support me, and still hold me accountable. When my dad sat across from the principal, with a big maple desk between them, he simply asked why I was so upset and why was he getting calls at work?

The principal responded that he was not sure why I was so upset, but he told my father that I had not qualified for Algebra 1; therefore, I had to take Grade 8 Math. My dad looked at the principal and clearly stated, "My son will be in Algebra 1 tomorrow, and you will make that happen." The principal exited the room, and I am sure today, to call the superintendent. My dad told me he would not be here if he didn't have complete confidence in me. No one will set limits on you, but you will work hard, do your best, and succeed.

The rest is history. The A that I received in Algebra 1 is entirely meaningless. The lesson that I learned that day—life-defining. I would not set limits on children! I would make sure school policies and procedures were not blocking students from high-level courses. I also would create advocacy systems for all students to succeed in our public schools. It is why becoming Superintendent of the Meriden Public Schools is my dream job!

In November of 1999, on Election Day, I became Mayor of Meriden, the city that meant so much to me. I worked as an assistant principal in a neighboring community while serving as Meriden's popularly elected mayor. At the time of my election, I was the youngest mayor in the state. Maybe the most naive as well. I was elected in a major upset; polls said that I would never win—I only knew children, and they can't vote.

Two lessons learned that day were first, my dad raised someone who is not afraid to lose, someone who will not give up, and second, when adults trust you with their children, they will trust you with anything—including their vote. As mayor, I acted as an educator; your heart does not change as your title does. In my fourth term as mayor, I stepped down to become principal of a high school in a neighboring town.

After two years as principal and three state championship teams, improved graduation rates, higher enrollment in advanced placement classes, and credit recovery for children in need of support, I was enjoying life and leadership. Though the inequities in education were so apparent, I wondered how a state and nation could sit idly. I knew public education was the key to my personal growth and success. I respected that public education was the great equalizer for me and believed it could be for the millions of students attending our nation's public schools.

As I became superintendent, I was committed to finding a way for public education to work for all students in America, like it did for me. As educational leaders are trying to level the playing field for all learners, the need for sound, tested, and tangible strategies for success could not be greater. Why does this matter? Why does this need to be our mission? Why does this matter so much to us?

For me, it is because my children Bria and Blake, who attend Meriden Public Schools, as well as all students attending public schools in America, deserve to be challenged every day in a school where they feel comfortable, supported, and prepared to succeed in a rapidly changing global society. What we want and expect for our children—what we want and expect for all children in our school system—are we willing to insist on the same for all children in America's public schools?

Acknowledgments

We would like to acknowledge our Meriden Public Schools' colleagues who have taught us that hard work is rewarding and fun: our central office team of Michael Grove, Louis Bronk, Patricia Sullivan-Kowalski, and Alvin Larson, whose work has provided much content for this book, and, more importantly, so many opportunities for our students and families. Thank you for making MPS a great place to work, laugh, and make a difference.

We would like to thank teacher union president Lauren Mancini-Averitt and former president Erin Benham for their true partnership, leadership, encouragement, and support. We would especially like to acknowledge Board of Education President Robert Kosienski, Jr., and former President Mark Hughes, as well as our terrific Board of Education, who guided the work, set goals to support all learners, embraced innovation, supported us always, and championed public education as the great equalizer.

We also want to acknowledge the following people who have helped us with this journey: Robert Angeli, Pete Civitello, Dan Corsetti, Dan Crispino, Brian Cyr, James Flynn, Tom Giard, Geoff Kenyon, Jeff Lund, Donna Mik, Susan Maffe, Rob Montemurro, Sue Moore, Sue Perrone, Evelyn Robles-Rivas, Victoria Ryan, David Salafia, Jen Straub, and Lysette Torres; as well as the foundations and consultants that have helped advance our work: Barr Foundation, Connecticut Association of Superintendents, Department of Education, Connecticut Center for School Change, Cormier Consulting, Coalition of Schools Educating Boys of Color, Education Development Center, Dalio Philanthropies/RISE Network, Education & Research, Nellie Mae Education Foundation, and Wallace Foundation.

Lastly, we want to acknowledge our students, staff, and families who have inspired us with their partnership, progress, and performance.

Authors' Notes

We are proud to be public school educators. We are proud to work in the most inclusive education system in the world. We are proud to work with all learners and their families. We are proud to have witnessed the power and impact of public education in America. We are proud to share their stories, their struggles, and their successes. Lastly, we are proud to share the six strategies we have used to ensure that American public education remains the Great Equalizer.

It was a late August evening, when a proud mother set out her young son's first day of school outfit. Tomorrow would be the start of the school year and the first day of kindergarten for this excited young child. As they got ready for the first day of school picture, dad was in his police officer uniform as he was preparing to go into work. This family lived in a small city in the central part of the state. The city was known for its silver manufacturing and faced many challenges like other former manufacturing cities across the nation. The city's public schools continued to be a source of pride and the home of opportunity.

Parents trusted their neighborhood public schools and knew that their children's future success was tied to their educational efforts. For this proud family, today was the start of their child's educational future. So, as they arrived at school, they were excited to say goodbye to their child and let the journey begin. However, their child greeted his first day of school with a fountain of tears and a leg hold on his mom as he had yet to learn English.

As the years passed, their student continued to experience success and joy throughout his elementary school experiences. The tears of the first day of kindergarten turned into tears of excitement, growth, learning, and plans to move on to middle school. These were years of public school success and then it was time to attend a public vocational high school. After high school, the student went to a public state university where he became a certified teacher. Immediately following graduation, he was hired as an elementary teacher back in his hometown.

Later, he became an instructional associate, principal, and assistant superintendent in the school system that helped raise him. This city was the home to a small, urban district where diversity was appreciated and all students respected. He led with empathy, compassion, and perseverance. So, who was this young child? This young child is our nation's Secretary of Education, Dr. Miguel Cardona.

Secretary Cardona grew up in Meriden, Connecticut, and was an assistant superintendent during our tenure. His educational career is a true story of how American public education can provide educational opportunities to ensure better lives for all children. For Dr. Cardona, public education was the great equalizer. We celebrate and dedicate this book to Dr. Cardona and all the students, staff, and families of the Meriden Public Schools who have guided our work, enriched our lives, and made this journey possible. They are the real testament that public education works in America.

We also dedicate this book to our families who have supported our work, encouraged our professional pursuits, and inspired us to dream.

I would like to dedicate this book to my mom, Gail, and my late father, Jack, who taught me the value of hard work, and the importance of treating all people the same regardless of status or circumstance, to Laura who provides so much love, support, and stability, and to my children Bria and Blake who amaze me every day with their work ethic, dedication to school and sports, and their loyalty to friends, classmates, and community.

—Mark Benigni

I dedicate this book to my parents, Bob and Shirley, who instilled in me that anything is possible, and my husband, Scott, who always encourages and supports me.

—Barbara Haeffner

I would like to dedicate this book to my family members who give me joy, happiness, and unfailing support: Jim and Linda and Jessica and Joey, Michael and Angela and Arden, Steve and Lucy, my late brother Ed, my forever sister in law Madelyne, and to my late husband Bruce—who was the best champion.

—Lois Lehman

Introduction

After working in and with public school districts, we identified six strategies that successful public education systems across our nation have implemented. We have confidence that today's educational leaders can help shape a new way that considers the needs of all of our diverse learners. While very few can argue with the need to improve achievement disparities, little consensus exists as to how. We offer a perspective here that combines the experiences of former teachers, school leaders, and district leaders, but more importantly, educators who have spent their lives improving public education for all students.

We are proud of our public school systems and the challenges they overcame on their journeys to success. Our school populations are microcosms of diverse communities where our students learn to live and work together in a natural setting reflective of today's society. Educators welcome the challenge of working in these school districts and the opportunities to make a difference in students' lives. These environments inspire mutual respect, encourage confidence, and build self-esteem. They set high expectations to ensure all students graduate high school and college, and are career-ready.

Are we willing to truly put our students at the center of our work? Do we recognize that high performing educational systems engage with partners in their greater communities? Our students, our nation, and the most inclusive educational system in the world are depending on all of us. Are we willing to stand up for the students and families who need us most? Join us as we share how you can be the great equalizer in your community by utilizing the six strategies that make public education work in America.

Success is not linear. We may not get it right the first time. The path to success will not be without obstacles. Change, uncertainty, and adjustments along the way are prerequisites for progress. Public education is our nation's path to ending poverty. While the path may have bumps, detours, and roadblocks along the way, we will change our schools and communities for the better with collaboration as our guide. Do not halt progress; come together to support strategies that work for all students in urban, suburban, and rural communities across our nation. This book aims to show the value of public education to the future of our nation and provide action steps for educators to follow. By learning from public education success stories, teachers, school leaders, board of education members, future educators, and those who recognize the importance of public education in America, we hope you will be inspired to take action. Together we can work to make public education even better for the next generation of students.

There are too few public education success stories being told; this book will provide a glimpse at how public education can work for students, staff, and families. As our nation is wrestling with health and social justice challenges, we need to hear the positive impact that public education can have on the lives of all students. Educators will benefit from learning six strategies that can be implemented to transform public school systems and offer hope to the students and families they serve every day.

This book provides the road map to ensure that public education in America remains the great equalizer for our students and families. All chapters will feature a hook, the actual story that humanizes the efforts and leaves us cheering for our students and staff. Chapters will also feature Key Takeaways, and Discussion Prompts to facilitate guided dialogue and reflective thought. Join us as we show how the hurdles and obstacles can be eliminated and the promise of American public education realized.

As schools are asked to do more and more with limited resources, the need for collaboration and partnerships is critical to the success of our public schools. Relationships with philanthropy and regional and national foundations can be leveraged to meet the growing needs of students, staff, and families. Partnerships with the press and media can provide a vehicle to highlight student and staff excellence. Partnerships matter!

The power of technology needs to be unleashed in our public schools. Technology can effectively personalize student learning, engage students, and provide all learners with immediate feedback and tangible goal targets. Make it less about the type of devices and insist that your students are 1:1. Ensure connectivity and integrate high-quality digital content into the core curriculum at all grade levels.

While there must be a strong commitment to increased academic performance, leaders should recognize the importance of embracing and nurturing the whole child and meeting their social-emotional needs as well. Racial awareness training for your staff addressing such areas as increasing racial consciousness, engaging in difficult conversations, and minimizing the impact of microaggressions and unconscious bias is critical.

Commit to meet the needs of those learners who count on you for support and are dependent on high-quality public education. By redesigning your education models for students needing special education services, you can improve learning opportunities for them. Support them with in-district programs while reallocating resources and savings to help all students achieve their dreams. Alignment of the curriculum for English Learners with the core subject area curricula will position students for academic and social-emotional success.

Be a district that truly assures that all students succeed and reach their full potential by challenging your highest performers with rigorous coursework and college readiness experiences. Eliminate barriers and guide your students down the road to success. The public school experience must provide students' academic and social-emotional skills to participate successfully in a global society. Every year provide your students with the opportunity to create new extracurricular and cocurricular activities that meet their needs, interests, and passions.

You can inspire your team by simply activating your personal leadership levers. With communities craving data and a nation guided by results, public schools must share all data transparently and publicly. As educators, we cannot make excuses. We face a significant challenge in public education in America—assuring that it is still the great equalizer. While a daunting task, we know we can and must keep that promise. Our children and our nation are depending on us.

Chapter 1

Building Partnerships
With All Stakeholders

A superintendent was a week into his new position, his dream job, superintendent of his hometown. Already, without a personnel director and an assistant superintendent, his personal assistant fell through her attic ceiling and shattered her leg. Yet, he remained optimistic; it could only get better. As he sorted through a pile of mail, he received a congratulatory note from one of his former students. How thoughtful, how sincere, and that is why he does this work—simply to make a difference in the lives of others.

Excited and feeling a sense of pride, he opened the next envelope. Could it be more encouraging news? He pulled the letter out of the envelope, he saw the official state seal, and he anxiously began to read the letter. But, unfortunately, the good news had run out, as this was the notice that if conditions did not improve at an elementary school, the state would be taking over the school. He was angry; this was not what he needed right now. Or was it? I was that superintendent and it was exactly what I needed at that moment. It would define my course of action over the next decade.

PARTNERING WITH YOUR TEAM

Decades ago, the relationship between school systems and their teachers' union could have been characterized as cold, distant, and distrusting. Unions spent most of their time fielding concerns and complaints from their members who believed they were not treated as professionals. Teachers had a minimal voice in instructional matters or in any initiatives that genuinely mattered. Teachers and building administrators struggled to resolve simple administrative issues like bell schedules, lunch duty, and room assignments.

Today, many unions and districts have developed strong partnerships that support teachers' focus on improving student achievement. Leadership must work closely with their local teachers' union. Union and management should contact each other weekly, and when necessary, sometimes daily, by a quick phone call, email, or text. Keep lines of communication open and be proactive rather than reactive.

Members of the union's executive board and central office leadership team need to be in close contact with each other. If the central office meets monthly, then once a month, the union leaders should join the central office monthly meeting to discuss new initiatives, share feedback, and be proactive in solving any potential issues. Labor-management collaboration must be in the DNA of school districts. The union should know it has the complete trust and respect of its central office team. School district leaders should work with them to move their districts forward together.

Implementing a comprehensive Talent Development System provides support for new teachers as they progress in their professional careers. A New Teacher Induction Program offers a venue for ongoing support sessions and learning about a district's vision, priorities, and initiatives. Peer Coaching pairs teachers to share best practices. Staff professional development encourages teachers to help design professional development days.

Leadership Academy builds capacity by engaging teacher leaders and aspiring administrators in specialized training programs and promoting year-long leadership projects implemented district wide or in their schools. Our Meriden Teachers Sharing Success (MTSS) also recognizes exemplary educators who provide support and growth opportunities for other classroom teachers.

Conducted in collaboration with the Connecticut Association of Schools, our district assembled a team prepared to meet our district's vision and initiatives. Elevating Director of Personnel to Assistant Superintendent for Personnel and Talent Development also brings importance to the district's talent development system. This position is responsible for continuing to develop programs that empower educators and create leadership opportunities for staff.

When our most needy elementary school was on the state's radar for a potential State Department of Education takeover, the central office and the union agreed that current student results were not acceptable. With that agreement in place, management and the union partners fended off state control and created internal accountability structures. The collaboration between management and labor spurred innovations and helped launch school improvement plans that worked.

First, the union president, principal, and superintendent met with the entire staff and explained that they could no longer accept the same dismal results year after year. They explained that if things did not improve, the school would be mandated to become a state oversight school. Teachers were notably

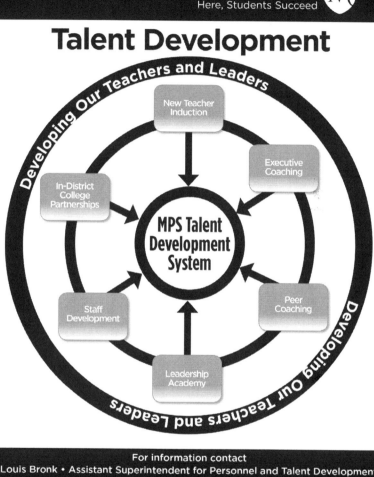

Figure 1.1. Talent Development. Meriden Public Schools, Meriden, CT

upset and unsure where to turn. So how did the district become a model that beat the odds and now is a school that the state encourages others to visit?

The district leadership team developed specific turnaround strategies focused on creating a sense of urgency, built buy-in from team members, placed the right people on the team, embraced engaging curriculum, utilized data from common assessments, and refused to blame students and families.

MERIDEN PUBLIC SCHOOLS
Here, Students Succeed

NEW TEACHER INDUCTION PROGRAM
A Comprehensive Approach to Supporting New Teachers

Three-Day New
Teacher Orientation

Mentor Program

CT TEAM Program

District Professional Learning Throughout the Year

- Meriden's Continuous Improvement
- Meriden Assessment System for Instruction
- CT TEAM Program
- Instructional Strategies
- PLC Data Teams
- Restorative Practices

- Creating a Positive Classroom Environment
- Teacher Evaluation
- Student-Centered Learning
- Blended-Learning Strategies
- School-based Professional Development
- ...and other topics

New Teacher Instructional Observation Walks

- Observation and discussion of instruction

Book Studies

- Growth Mindset, Carol Dweck
- Classroom Management That Works, Robert Marzano
- Lost at School, Ross W. Greene

Interactive Online New Teacher Discussion Forum

- On Google Classroom

For questions about joining the Meriden Team, contact Louis Bronk
Assistant Superintendent for Personnel and Talent Development • louis.bronk@meridenk12.org

22 Liberty Street, Meriden CT 06450 | 203-630-4209 | www.meridenk12.org

Figure 1.2. New Teacher Induction Program. Meriden Public Schools, Meriden, CT

Staff additions and community partnerships led to a positive climate with a reenergized faculty of enthusiastic and dedicated teachers, supportive staff, and community partners with high expectations for all students.

The district and union committed to belief statements for parents. The three essential belief statements became the theory of action:

- Increased student achievement and high expectations for all are necessities that will be achieved in a no-blame culture.
- Additional learning opportunities filled with engaging, personalized, technology-rich learning will lead to greater student success.
- Increased attendance and improved school climates promote higher academic performance, creating schools where students and staff want to be.

Led by staff and community partners, our district capitalized on improving school cultures and redoubled efforts to establish a culture of high expectations. A review of school student performance data indicated significant underperformance in key student academic indicators. Equally concerning were the high chronic absenteeism rate and the number of suspensions. Transformation strategies were needed that encompassed leadership, teaching and learning, professional development, curriculum and assessment, climate, and parental partnerships.

This meant having courageous conversations with teachers and school-based administration; ultimately, this meant ensuring that staff was all in this together. Recognizing that teachers and administrators are being asked to implement changes that require learning new skills, adopting new practices, and implementing new leadership strategies, we were prepared to provide extensive professional development to support personalized learning for staff. Academic interventions included additional reading, math, and special education support.

To build the home-school partnership in establishing high expectations for students, a Family School Liaison Team was created. One of our Family School Liaisons was assigned to work with parents providing wraparound services, including home visits to support families. With our student-centered team in place, high expectations for all, and actively engaged stakeholders, the school was braced for success. Concurrently, the district worked collaboratively with the union to identify and apply for grant funding opportunities.

A highly competitive American Federation of Teachers (AFT) Innovation Grant provided students with 100 additional minutes of instruction and enrichment each day—the equivalent of 40 additional school days. Union and management agreed to pay teachers a stipend to work longer hours and allow community partners to work side by side with our teachers and students during the new recognized school day. Innovations included staggered teacher work schedules, teacher stipends, use of outside providers in the school, and teacher transfers without a side letter or memorandum of understanding.

The creativity and flexibility that resulted from this true collaboration were astounding. It is just one example of the power of a district, a teachers' union, and community partners coming together to make a bold, productive idea a successful reality for students and teachers. Districts should welcome

FAMILY-SCHOOL LIAISON TEAM

Connecting Schools, Families, and Our Community

Spelling Bee at Senior Center   Author Avi at Lincoln Middle School   Enrichment Program at Israel Putnam

THE FAMILY-SCHOOL LIAISONS (FSLs):

- USE comprehensive services that engage parents as partners by promoting numerous parent leadership activities.

- WORK cooperatively with students, adult family members, school staff, and community partners to promote active family partnerships, PBIS, and great attendance rewards.

- REMOVE barriers that prevent students from learning, such as supporting JAD program, monitoring chronic absences, and providing alternatives to suspensions and expulsions.

- PROVIDE students with proactive preventative services which promote success, utilizing community partners such as DCF, CHC, Boys & Girls Club, Beat the Street, the Y, and the NAACP.

- ENSURE effective targeted family interactions through 1 on 1 home visits and supportive advocacy at PPTs.

EXAMPLES OF OUR WORK:

- Visiting Authors

- Family activities at our schools and throughout our community

- Welcome bags for all new families

- On-line referral system

- Million Word Reader Celebration

THANK YOU TO ALL OF OUR COMMUNITY PARTNERS!

For more information, assistance, or to partner with us, please call (203) 630-4423

Figure 1.3. Family School Liaison Team. Meriden Public Schools, Meriden, CT

the opportunity to partner with their unions and teacher groups around shared goals for their students and schools. When partnerships place students first, communities will have greater value and respect for their schools. Unions must support their members but all successful collaborations must prioritize the students, families, and communities they serve.

Within five years, the school was considered a model by the state, chosen as a Model Community School by the International Center for Leadership in

Education, and selected by the US Department of Education as a National Blue Ribbon School. When students, staff, and families work together, believe in all children, increase learning time, embrace technology tools and not accept failure—schools can beat the odds and assure that—Here, All Students Succeed.

The Meriden Public Schools' ongoing work with our teacher union was recognized when our union president and the superintendent received a joint award for collaboration from the American Federation of Teachers (AFT), Connecticut. Our partnership was featured in the AFT American Educator, "Moving Meriden: A Road Map for Union-District Relationships." It was the first time in over 30 years that the award was presented to a superintendent and a union president for district-union relationships.

We must stand up for our public education systems and the dedicated teachers who make a difference every day. They chose to spend their careers in our public schools, and we should respect their commitment. We can't let society blame our teachers and their unions for all of our nation's challenges and inequities. Talk with students and families, and you will see the positive impact an educator can have on a student's life. We are inspired by the work that public school educators are doing every day to support students and families.

- Key Takeaway: Union management relationships matter. Invite your union leaders to meet with your central office leadership team monthly.

PARTNERING WITH YOUR FAMILIES

What do you want your schools to be? When districts asked their students, parents/guardians, and families, their answers were consistent. They want schools that inspire, are safe and orderly, challenge and support, and provide additional services. For too long, parental involvement has meant attendance at school events and volunteerism; in essence, parent seat time. The new concept of community and family involvement must go beyond attendance and volunteerism. The focus must be on improved student achievement, budget allocations, community engagement, and respect for public education.

Families and community providers need to be active partners in education, student advocates, and public school supporters to increase student achievement. They must ensure that outside school conditions support student learning. High-quality and high-performing schools have strong partnerships with their students' families and the larger community. Supporting education outside the school walls is the best predictor of student academic success and high school completion. Technology can expand learning time for students and create a more robust academic connection between school and home.

So how do you get beyond family engagement as volunteerism? An effective strategy is implementing a Family-School Liaison (FSL) Program, which engages parents in their children's educational success and the initiatives of the school district. The FSL Coordinator is supported by a group of bilingual family-school liaisons who make home visits, facilitate proactive family engagement, foster school and community relationships, and plan creative student and family engagement events. Parent breakfasts, fan buses, guest author visits, and intergenerational spelling bees are just a few of the creative ways an FSL team engages students and families.

To be competitive in the 21st century and beyond, students need to attain life and career skills, communication and social skills, and technology skills. It is up to the education community to make sure our parents/guardians and community members are informed, ready, and able to support our students. The FSL Program is designed to help provide and encourage that level of support. These community and family partnerships will help students achieve higher grades and test scores, improve attendance, improve behavior at home and school, achieve higher levels of learning, and be more career and life ready at graduation.

Engaged citizens have a stronger sense of respect and support from and toward the school, improved awareness of student progress, a greater appreciation of a teacher's work, and increased feelings of partnership with their schools. Engaged parents/guardians and community members are a benefit for teachers as well. Teachers will have an increased awareness of student success factors, greater readiness to involve families, greater use of community resources, and increased satisfaction with teaching.

All communities have hopes and dreams for their children, all communities can contribute to their children's education, and all communities can help "be the difference." Community agencies, families, and school staff can be true partners in education. This approach should be a practical strategy for a public school system. Do community and parent partnerships matter in your school district? Will funds be invested during difficult economic times in community partnership programs? Are you ready to partner with your families for student success?

School districts, parents, and community members are rightfully concerned with their students' ability to become collaborative members of society, their home community, and their schools. Schools must open their doors to community partners and engage parents and community members. If public schools are to be successful, then dedicated teachers, with the support of religious groups, community, and civic organizations, and parents must collaboratively work and guide students down their path to success. We can make this happen with full-service community schools that have progressive partnership strategies for families.

- Key Takeaway: Create a diverse Family School Liaison Team who can do proactive outreach and engagement with your students and families.

PARTNERING WITH LOCAL SERVICE PROVIDERS

Too often, schools are helping to support families with raising children, taking on many of the roles traditionally belonging to parents. In a more complex and fast-paced world, today's teens are growing up more quickly than teens of a generation ago. If schools are to meet these new challenges, they must actively engage the community with the school and the school with the community. They must find ways to teach young people how to be good leaders and give them meaningful opportunities for authentic leadership, school involvement, and community service.

Open your schools to reputable entities that can help support students and families. Your schools can become community schools, full-service hubs of activity for school initiatives to flourish, and community service providers to positively impact students. Community schools offer expanded learning opportunities, customized programs to meet the goals of their target neighborhood, and social services for students and their families. Many districts have embraced the community school concept, brought in outside partners to help students and their families, and implemented open access policies.

Community partners with security-screened employees can work with a school system to provide services to improve the educational outcomes of our students. This design welcomes school resource officers in schools, operating community health centers in school buildings, providing office hours at schools for child guidance clinics, and partnering with local community agencies to provide the support that our parents and students require.

A true sense of community is evident in many districts that have implemented academic programs and social gatherings for parents/guardians to build connections with families and community providers. While these programs are showing promise to maintain strong and vibrant partnerships, districts need to remain fully committed to seeking new approaches to ensure that family and community partnerships are significant components of their district improvement plans and continuous improvement system.

Community schooling is not just another program being imposed on a school building. It is a way of thinking, acting, and doing business that recognizes the central role that communities and families play in children's education and the power of working together. Schools have closer relationships with young people and their families than many other community organizations do. Community agencies must help families and schools raise happy, healthy, and well-educated members of society.

For their part, schools must open their doors and seek out parents and other adults, neighborhood businesses, local outreach programs, and community agencies. Schools that respect their partners and involve them in meaningful youth-focused activities have better results. It is not enough to say to a young person that you should become a leader. We must provide the training, support, and opportunities that teens need to help them become the leaders of tomorrow.

One way to do this is through after-school activities. Many teens recognize the benefits of co-curricular programming and want a safe place to go after school where they can feel comfortable and connected. A student in need of an adult support network can find that support in programs offered by numerous community partners. School-community partnerships can be successful when they operate at low cost and adapt to the community's changing needs.

Community partners provide staffing and specialized enrichment activities while working side by side with teachers in before and after-school programs. Teachers can partner with community agencies to provide enrichment activities that improve student engagement and offer underserved populations opportunities to experience cultural activities deepening their background knowledge.

Teens need to be excited about a program if it is going to be successful. They need to accept the responsibility for running it and be willing to put in the time and effort required to ensure program success. If we want to understand our teens, we must allow them to share their interests with us in a judgment-free forum. And we must recognize that, given the guidance and support of the community, our young people can make a positive and significant impact.

- Key Takeaway: Community school models can successfully connect local service providers with students and families who benefit from their support.

PARTNERING WITH YOUR MUNICIPALITY

As school superintendents, boards of education, mayors, municipal leaders, and health officials worked together to keep schools, businesses, and community organizations open during the pandemic, communities and their citizens were looking for leadership committed to success. During these challenging times, honest, transparent, and collaborative leadership is essential. These new and unprecedented challenges have provided all of us an opportunity for progress, a pathway for partnerships, and the confidence to confront conflicts head on and collaboratively.

School systems committed to continuous improvement realize it is all about partnerships. Working together, we can and must do more. The pandemic challenges helped districts make significant progress in learning important lessons about shared governance and collaborative partnerships. It encouraged Boards of Education to adopt new policies, stand up to public pressure, and commit to open and positive relationships.

Successful leaders invented new strategies and found new techniques to coordinate service for their students, staff, and families. These changes offer hope and provide direction to our public education school systems. These leaders saw the end goal of community success and were willing to share power and promote partnerships to gain positive outcomes for their students, staff, and families. These changes offer hope and provide direction to our public education school systems.

For years, city departments have operated independently of the superintendent's office and their local school boards. The pandemic challenges provided an opportunity to support the comprehensive needs of a community from public health, safety, and education. Through this partnership, resources could be shared in a timely, cost-effective manner. With the problem identified, the progress underway, and the path cleared, it is now time to share these successes.

How do we know that shared governance and enhanced partnerships have benefited communities in their successful efforts to ensure school and student success? Evidence that partnerships between municipalities and boards of education are working and communities are meeting the challenges of the pandemic, racial unrest, and education inequality are visible in the following multiple departmental partnerships:

- City Leadership and Governance
    - Superintendents of Schools participate in weekly briefings with all city department heads.
    - Superintendents share proactive solutions to potential issues that impact students and families.
- Health and Human Services
    - Local health and human services conduct COVID-19 contact tracing and monitoring of students and staff.
    - Local health and human services provide school leaders with accurate, timely data facilitating daily communication.
- Community Health Center

Community health centers provide behavioral health, medical, and
dental services.
School-based health clinics in our neighborhood public schools pro-
vide preventive services.
- Economic Development
Schools must partner with local community agencies to provide
before and after-school care for students.
Community agencies can provide enrichment activities for students.
- Community Development
Food service distribution must be available throughout the commu-
nity for all learners.
Families should be made aware of free Wi-Fi locations in the com-
munity, the availability of Wi-Fi hotspots, and low-cost internet
options.
- Fire Department
Fire department engages in reviewing and endorsing ventilation in
buildings.
Fire department inspects outdoor classroom tents to ensure appropri-
ate safety procedures are in place.
- Police Force
Police force cooperation and involvement with the schools help maintain social distance at school events and on school grounds.
School Resource Officer (SRO) programs provide a vehicle for school
and police collaboration.

Districts are using SRO programs creatively and have moved beyond traditional policing. The SRO program has brought the community into the school
and the school into the community. The SROs are active in all aspects of the
school day and build relationships with students and staff. In this new environment, police officers work collaboratively with students and staff to plan
events and activities. Having a community member who is a professional
working in your high school enhances the climate and culture of the building.

SRO officers located at middle and high schools can provide law-related
counseling and teaching. Classroom presentations may include a Civics class
presentation on the Fourth Amendment which protects unreasonable searches
and seizures by the government, current law-related events, and career opportunities in criminal justice. SROs also work with students in crisis. Daily, they
join students in the cafeteria, where they have opportunities to interact with
students informally.

Educators can leverage SROs as an additional resource to provide students
needed support. When educators and police personnel share their knowledge
and expertise, relationships are formed, students are best served, education

is enhanced, and communities are strengthened. After all, successful schools have a positive climate where students are involved and feel connected to the adults in the building.

- Key Takeaway: Shared governance models built on respect and trust can improve services for students.

PARTNERING FOR SUCCESS WITH PHILANTHROPIC ORGANIZATIONS

As public schools deal with shrinking public aid and constant public scrutiny over funding, they should garner an ally from the foundations that have previously partnered exclusively with charter schools and private schools. With many charter schools showing inconsistent results and many others performing below their community's public schools, savvy educational foundations are rethinking their investment strategy and funding public school systems committed to innovation, equity, access, and success for all students.

Public school systems must support innovation and collaboration and respect and partner with outside agencies and education foundations if they are serious about securing support from philanthropy. Our diverse public school populations make it more important than ever before that the playing field is leveled for all of our students and that all graduates have a plan for the future. Foundation support and grant opportunities will become available to public schools willing to open their doors to these new partners.

Our district created student-centered learning environments, where all students were given voice and choice in creating their personalized learning pathway. This student-first focus helped the district achieve their highest test scores in district history, as well as their highest graduation rates. This program was funded with significant dollars and technical support from a well-known regional educational foundation.

Grade nine on-track and college career readiness are innovative initiatives that other public schools have received grant funding from foundations. At-risk ninth graders are grouped in small cohorts and supported by transition support specialists to ensure they stay on track and advance to tenth grade. Students who need additional support require school staff to regularly review academic data, attendance records, and behavioral reports. These efforts greatly increased the percentages of all ninth graders currently on track to graduate in four years.

Data reveal that effective principals are a significant lever to school success. One district is working closely with its state university system and a foundation to ensure that all educational leaders have the data they need and an action plan in place to drive school improvement. Public school partnerships with foundations open up a realm of meaningful relationships outside the traditional K-12 educational setting.

Public school districts can be "true" partners, engage in honest conversations, welcome visitors into their schools and classrooms, and foster authentic dialogues with their staff and stakeholders, including valued philanthropies. Public schools that enter into a partnership may face many unknowns, but it can be an exciting, challenging, and rewarding journey. As public funding remains unstable with political leadership changes and an ever-revolving economic picture, foundation influence on our nation's education policy and practices will remain constant.

How do we make people aware and highlight that some of the most creative work in education occurs in public schools across our nation? As public schools build relationships and celebrate success, they will open up new opportunities for their students and staff. When we open the doors to our public schools and share the successes of our students and staff, those foundations committed to high-quality education and equal opportunities for all will recognize the importance of investing in our public schools.

- Key Takeaway: Just because some foundations have traditionally partnered with charter schools and private reform networks, welcome their support to your public school system if their resources are aligned to their mission.

PARTNERING WITH HIGHER EDUCATION

Creating lasting partnerships will require a K-20 focus on education. We will strengthen relationships with K-12 and higher education by looking at a student's educational journey from kindergarten through four years of post-high school work. As technology transforms society and our schools, it becomes more important that our school systems and colleges work together. Our public K-12 education systems and higher education institutions must place students at the center of the work and realize that their mutual success will directly impact our nation's collective growth and progress. The time is now; our students need us to get it right!

When K-12 and higher education have true partnerships and do not simply pass the blame and point fingers, our students succeed. Reading, math, critical thinking, regular attendance, and social comfort are skills that our students need when preparing for college. Stressing the importance of social-emotional stability, academic rigor, and perseverance/grit will increase students attending college and, more importantly, graduating from college.

Educators must value and respect student engagement and personal learning interests at all grade levels. By recognizing the unique talents of all learners, educators will build the relationships necessary to encourage students to challenge themselves in rigorous courses. That is how we will create a K-20 system that grows our nation's economy and improves our communities.

Partner with your local community college. A community college branch was placed in an innovative district's high school because of the district's partnership with the local Community College Foundation. The district receives five tuition-free seats in all classes for its students and staff in exchange for free teaching space. The opportunity to enroll in college courses at their school, earn free college credits, and gain experience with challenging college coursework are exciting options for their high school students.

Another district benefited from partnerships with higher education that placed interns and student teachers in their schools. This district also offered degree programs in their school buildings for their staff to have the convenience of college classes located right at the schools in which they teach. Administrators and teachers interested in advanced degrees saved time and effort by not having to travel to a college. This resulted in benefiting both students, the district, and the college.

- Key Takeaway: Offer college credit-earning classes for your students during and after-school hours and open up your facilities to higher education institutions.

PARTNERING WITH THE PRESS, MEDIA, AND BUSINESS COMMUNITY

Every public school district has something they and their communities are proud of—something special, something unique, something making a difference for their students, staff, and stakeholders. Put pen to paper or power up your laptop and tell how you led your public school district to success; sharing your district's success road map could lead others to seek out and try new ideas and programs.

Do not be afraid to share your best practices, your successes, as well as the challenges you know await you and your team. National, regional, and state conferences are anxious to highlight the fantastic work occurring in your schools. Work with your team to assemble a presentation proposal that highlights your schools and staff. Be sure to include classroom teachers and students in your presentation, as audiences are always interested in what they have to say.

Simply applying will validate the work, build team morale, and instill a district sense of pride. When the first acceptance letter arrives, you will energize your team and continue to support their professional growth as well. Staff welcomes the perspectives and lessons learned of other districts and enjoy the intellectual stimulation that a conference brings. Conference attendance, session participation, and conversations with other educators might lead to your own district's next innovation.

Successful public school districts regularly present at major national, regional, and state events. Encourage your team to honor your students by applying for state, regional, and national recognition. Your students, staff, and stakeholders deserve it. Nothing is more rewarding for a local Board of Education than to be presented with a plaque, trophy, or symbol of their district's efforts and success.

From Fortune 500 companies to regional vendors to neighborhood family stores, businesses invest in marketing because they see it as an important component of their sustainability, growth, and development plan. Public school districts, from urban cities to rural communities, should consider capitalizing on district marketing campaigns. Do not let public outcry deter you from using tax dollars to highlight your district, schools, and students.

As private schools, charter schools, and colleges have realized, it is a wise short-term and long-term investment. These schools typically have well-orchestrated marketing campaigns to compete for tuition-based school students successfully. Attractive flyers, social media efforts, television commercials, redesigned websites, and other digital marketing initiatives should be considered by public school districts serious about effectively branding their district.

Our public schools are facing competition for their students and the money that private providers hope will follow. Do not let charter schools, private schools, and religious schools in your neighboring communities recruit your brightest, most involved students. Tell your story, market your innovations, and dispel the myth that public schools cannot be pioneering leaders in ensuring success for all students.

Let your outreach team assist the district with their marketing efforts as they know the community and its stakeholders. Use multiple marketing strategies to highlight and promote the great work being done in your schools. Brand a consistent logo and color schemes on all signage and your new, improved website. Consider a student-focused theme for your district that is engaging to students and appealing to families. Make sure your new theme appears with your district logo and web address on all print materials and online resources.

Create an inclusive theme that will appear on brochures, school signs, clothing apparel, school vehicles, student giveaways, and student and district awards. Electronic billboards and TV commercials that can be shown on local cable stations and viewed on major networks will expand your reach to include all stakeholders. Your local movie theater may be willing to donate ad time to air your district's commercial. Students and families will take great pride in your district's new brand once they notice your efforts.

School districts must develop, maintain, and build their own successful brand to engage internal and external audiences. Your students, staff, families, and elected leaders might be a receptive group with which to start. These people not only want to help you share your success stories, but they are also the ones who are most proud. So, provide them with positive data, success sound bites, and let them share what you are doing with the public. Keep it simple and share specific data points with elected leaders and your local school board. Find time at board meetings to honor and celebrate students and staff for academics and innovation.

Reward your students and staff with special recognitions for being top performers in your district. Your teachers' union can sponsor programs recognizing high achievement in elementary, middle, and high school and honor students at district ceremonies. Students and staff can be featured on promotional flyers in your local newspaper and displayed prominently on your website. Student-recommended guest speakers and nationally recognized authors can encourage student interest in reading. Share examples of students being digital learners, as these are also the celebrations that your families and media are excited to share with the public.

Your external audience comprises community not-for-profits, local businesses, regional and national companies who do business with your district, and local restaurants, stores, and service industries that your students and families frequent. Provide opportunities for your external audience to participate in school events and spend time with your students and families. Concerts, sports contests, theater, and shows allow businesses to see your best salespeople—your students. Provide free passes to school athletic events and concerts to seniors and veterans who reside in your community.

Bring the community and parents into your high schools to see firsthand how learning has changed. Bring business leaders, community providers, nonprofit agencies, and parents into your classrooms. Let them see blended learning in action through community and parent learning walk sessions. Districts have started using a learning walks protocol, a rubric for reflection on teaching and learning, to guide a school's continuous improvement efforts. This protocol is utilized by teachers, administrators, and guests when they visit classrooms together.

Build capacity and shared ownership by empowering educators to assist you in the continuous improvement and development process. This collegial model is designed for observing, collaborating, providing feedback,

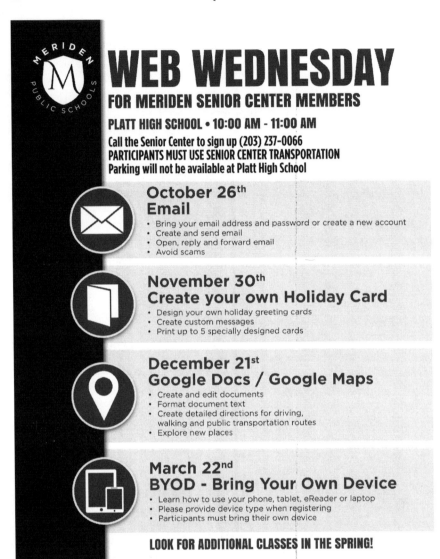

WEB WEDNESDAY

FOR MERIDEN SENIOR CENTER MEMBERS

PLATT HIGH SCHOOL • 10:00 AM - 11:00 AM

Call the Senior Center to sign up (203) 237-0066
PARTICIPANTS MUST USE SENIOR CENTER TRANSPORTATION
Parking will not be available at Platt High School

October 26th
Email
• Bring your email address and password or create a new account
• Create and send email
• Open, reply and forward email
• Avoid scams

November 30th
Create your own Holiday Card
• Design your own holiday greeting cards
• Create custom messages
• Print up to 5 specially designed cards

December 21st
Google Docs / Google Maps
• Create and edit documents
• Format document text
• Create detailed directions for driving,
  walking and public transportation routes
• Explore new places

March 22nd
BYOD - Bring Your Own Device
• Learn how to use your phone, tablet, eReader or laptop
• Please provide device type when registering
• Participants must bring their own device

LOOK FOR ADDITIONAL CLASSES IN THE SPRING!

Figure 1.4. Web Wednesday. Meriden Public Schools, Meriden, CT

sharing classroom strategies, reflecting, and improving student outcomes. Encouraging collaboration at all levels can empower teachers to improve teaching and learning and break down the barriers of isolation.

Do not forget to include your local senior citizens in your school's outreach efforts. Our district developed a monthly Web Wednesday event so senior citizens from their Senior Center could engage with high school students and learn technical skills in their school's 21st century learning environments. These senior citizens quietly become their best ambassadors in the community. A Take Charge and Code event held by another school brought families who joined together to program robotic mice and explore pocket robots. Virtual reality demonstrations included swimming with dolphins, exploring space, touring another nation, and other topics.

Create a Community Support Award for your Board of Education to honor and show appreciation to key community partners who give back to your students and schools. Recognize partners such as the pizza place that gives a free slice to students who make the honor roll, the barbershop that offers free haircuts to students for participating in sports, or the ice cream shop that celebrates students for their community service.

These business partners and community partners can be recognized with a small plaque at televised school board meetings. This recognition, welcomed by recipients, will encourage other business partners to become involved with their public schools. When participating in these types of outreach programs, make sure you reinforce your district's brand and celebrate your students, staff, staff, and helpful partners.

Promote your middle and high schools with promotional videos and flyers. Invite transitioning fifth and eighth graders into your schools to learn what their public schools have to offer to them. Despite competition from private and charter schools, you will find that few families will choose to leave your district when they see all that their public schools have to offer. Market special education programs in a similar fashion.

While promotional videos and catchy brochures should be considered, do not underestimate how school tours, where parents and students see learning from their own viewpoint, can have a positive effect on student selection. A comprehensive approach is how you will convince parents and guardians to keep their children in your district. Keeping students in their neighborhood public schools saves millions of community tax dollars for your community groups and helps build stronger schools and communities.

Your local community has groups such as Rotary Club, Lions Club, Kiwanis Club, the NAACP, Jaycees, Chamber of Commerce, and others that are interested in hearing your district's story and supporting your schools. Speak at luncheons or dinners for these local groups. Always be available to local media so your voice can be heard and accurate reports shared. Open your doors to the news media. Let them visit your schools so they can share school events, student successes, and staff awards with the public. Take a minute to send an informational email to a local media outlet, alerting them to school events as there is no harm if they do not show up.

Develop a system wide marketing campaign for your schools, encompassing both internal and external audiences. Inform your partners about every

Meriden Public Schools'
Community Support Award

Presented to

Gallery 53

In Grateful Appreciation

For Outstanding Support

To the Meriden Public Schools' Students

In Recognition of Our Community Partners

The Meriden Board of Education

Figure 1.5. Community Support Award. Meriden Public Schools, Meriden, CT

one of your new programs and invite them to participate in your school community's activities. A two-way relationship where your partners support and celebrate student success with you will ensure sustainability and continue to keep the focus on the great work of your students and staff.

- Key Takeaway: Always be proud to share the good work of your students and staff.

WHY PARTNERSHIPS MATTER

Successful partnerships ensure that leaders from all sectors maintain close and trusting relationships that collectively push strategic and community-driven plans for improvement. As our nation's cities and public schools are asked to do more, let the partnerships established and the progress realized offer a brighter future for our students, schools, and communities. The best leaders recognize that it is all about partnerships, and they work hard to build them. They see American public education as the great equalizer.

- Key Takeaway: We can't do it alone, but together we can.

DISCUSSION PROMPTS

How are you maximizing partnerships?
What new partnerships can be formed?
Do your families feel welcome at your schools?
How do you connect with higher education?
How do you showcase your work to the greater community?

Chapter 2

Leveraging Technology for Learning

Maria was a single mom who came to the United States from Aguada, Puerto Rico, when she was 23. She worked at a local candy factory by day and at an area shopping mall at night. Her son, Manuel, attended his neighborhood public school, where he embraced technology and science instruction. So, in addition to the box of chocolates waiting for Manuel, a couple of neatly wrapped presents were placed on the table next to his birthday cake. As he opened the first box, he shook it, tilted it from side to side, questioned its weight, and, then like any good scientist, gave his best hypothesis.

Manuel guessed that it was a new science book that he wanted about animals of the Amazon. After researching the Amazon, Manuel was fascinated and hoped someday to visit. You can only imagine Maria's excitement as Manuel opened the box's front cover and slowly pulled back the paper. After all, Maria had been saving for months for this special gift. Manuel's gift was a tablet, and now a whole new world was opened up to him. While he might not visit the Amazon anytime soon, he certainly will virtually!

THE REALITY

American educators recognize the importance of public education in breaking the cycle of poverty and leveling the playing field for all students. Public education is especially critical in a global society that will necessitate a workforce with the requisite communication, collaboration, critical thinking, and creativity skills. Knowing that children with fewer resources deserve an educational system that provides them with tools for the jobs of the 21st century and beyond, districts must embark on a digital transformation.

Over a decade ago, with no district-issued devices and other districts with policies that banned devices, our small urban district knew that it had to garner buy-in from all stakeholders if it was going to launch its transformation successfully. The district knew it had to respect its students, staff, and families as it was asking them to make significant shifts in their current knowledge base and regular comfort zones. The district realized it had to get devices into the hands of students, and the quickest way to do that was by letting them use the ones they were already bringing to school with them every day.

Working with their Board of Education, our district developed Bring Your Own Device (BYOD) Guidelines to support the use of student devices. Teachers were eager to try a different approach and maximize the technology students brought to school. Rather than spending their time taking devices away from students, teachers began incorporating them into classroom learning. To generate interest, the district sponsored community forums for students to showcase the educational benefits of technology as they garnered support from community stakeholders. Students also presented the value of technology in their learning at Board of Education meetings.

Teachers quickly dispelled the myth that they would open a Pandora's box by allowing students to bring their own devices to school. To their credit, they expanded their classroom walls and embraced new possibilities. With district guidance and high-level activities prepared, students became more responsible and engaged in their learning. As a result of the BYOD implementation, the district realized that not all students had a device to bring to school. Students often shared a family device, some students did not have a device at all, and limited data plans proved to be a hurdle when accessing digital content learning activities.

With the Board of Education's full support, the district examined its priorities and looked closely at the allocation of resources to identify areas for cost savings to purchase devices for all learners. The district reallocated the cost of pencils and paper, textbooks, and consultants to devices, digital content, and in-house trainers. Within 10 years, the district went from having zero devices to a truly 1:1 learning environment and, now today, operates in a 2:1 and in some cases 3:1 learning environment. Providing these components was essential as the district's digital transformation leveraged technology and enhanced learning.

Devices and connectivity were the building blocks for the transformation. Next, the district sought out and developed strategic partnerships with high-quality digital content providers. The new digital content provides engaging, self-paced, differentiated instruction that fosters independent learning. Provider partnerships allowed more significant opportunities to support equitable education for all students and professional learning for teachers. Through digital content, teachers adapted instruction so that students were now challenged at their own academic levels. Students were also able to access learning opportunities anytime and anywhere.

The Board of Education supported the district's digital transformation by reviewing, revising, and developing district policy and goals to put students at the center. The Board of Education adopted the following learning goals:

- To provide a student-centered learning environment to meet the individual needs of each student according to their specific background, capabilities, learning style, interests, and aspirations;
- To provide an educational program that will lead to college and career readiness for all students;
- To provide technology and a resource-rich learning environment; and
- To provide opportunities for learning outside the traditional classroom and school building (e.g., online courses, independent study, internships, and externships).

With the Board's full support and commitment, the district was on its way. While teachers were open to using educational technology and willing to try, as with any new technology, there was a steep learning curve and indeed some apprehension. As a district that valued collaboration and personal growth, its teachers welcomed and embraced high-quality professional learning opportunities, primarily when delivered by their colleagues. One of its greatest successes was the staff's willingness to realize they needed to teach differently, to motivate and engage students in personalized learning experiences.

The district developed a Look Fors document, a self-reflective instrument for teachers to assess student-centered learning in their classrooms and their student work. The district provided personalized professional learning opportunities for staff by embedding in-house technology specialists to provide daily coaching and support at the school, summer drop-in sessions, lunch and learns, and tiered workshops. Teachers were able to self-select their learning environment based on the level of comfort and expertise that best fit their needs.

"I'm Charged" teachers are leading the digital transition and are recognized for their innovative classroom practices. These teacher leaders demonstrate effective use of technology to promote deeper learning and increase student choice and voice opportunities. They are the early adopters, positive influencers, and "go-to" experts in their buildings, as they share best practices with their peers. Their classrooms are exemplary models for colleagues to visit, sharing new learning, and implementing new strategies and programs.

Administrators enrolled in online courses to ensure they were comfortable supporting their teaching staff in an online learning environment. They assumed the role of students and participated in self-paced, multi-modal experiences, which provided them with an understanding of blended learning. Even the youngest students are supporting one another. Tech Buddies pairs

Defining Student-Centered Learning

Student-Centered Learning is an approach to planning and delivering instruction that promotes student voice, ownership, and opportunities for students to make learning decisions. Student-centered learning engages students in their own success, incorporates their interests and skills into the learning process and encourages students to take responsibility for their learning. Student-centered learning requires intentionally designed lessons to ensure authenticity and relevance of student learning experiences. Lessons are personalized and students are guided to deeper levels of understanding. The role of the teacher shifts along a continuum, whereby the teacher increasingly becomes the facilitator and contributor of the learning process rather than the director of knowledge.

The principles of *Student-Centered Learning* are:
- Student Ownership Over Their Learning
- Personalized Learning
- Anytime, Anywhere Learning
- Mastery-Based Learning

Student Ownership Over Their Learning

Student Ownership Over Their Learning involves engaging students in their own success by providing opportunities for students to reflect, self-regulate and improve. Students are provided tools to address habits of mind and growth-oriented mindsets. Students understand that they have multiple pathways to success. Teacher supports students' abilities to advocate and make decisions about their learning. Student voice is encouraged and used in planning and demonstration of mastery.

Personalized Learning

Personalized Learning involves designing learning opportunities with student interests and academic needs at the center. Personalized learning is student-driven and individually paced. Instruction incorporates student choice, ownership and differentiated tasks. Learning is deepened and reinforced through technology integration, participation in collaborative group work, and a focus on engaging and increasingly complex and authentic problems and projects.

Anytime, Anywhere Learning

Anytime, Anywhere Learning extends beyond the traditional school day. Authentic use of technology allows for flexibility with respect to time and place and provides opportunities for students to direct their learning. Students have multiple opportunities to demonstrate their acquisition of skills and knowledge.

Mastery-Based Learning

Mastery-Based Learning allows students to progress through the curriculum at an individualized pace upon mastery of key learning targets. Students have multiple opportunities and means to demonstrate mastery through performance and cooperative tasks. Students are provided choice and autonomy. Lessons are scaffolded and differentiated to meet individual needs and learning profiles.

Adapted from NMEF *Putting Students at the Center* Reference Guide.

Figure 2.1a.

younger students with older students at the elementary level, allowing mentors to share their technical expertise across grade levels. As teachers' roles evolve into facilitators, students take greater ownership of their learning and become content creators and technology advocates.

District implementation of a single sign-on, Google Workspace, and designation as a Google Reference District can further empower teachers to

Student-Centered Learning Look Fors

Teacher Look Fors	Student Look Fors
Student Ownership Over Their Learning	
▪ Providing students with reflective prompts or tools ▪ Structuring activities that allow for student input ▪ Encouraging students to persevere ▪ Providing growth-oriented feedback ▪ Structuring higher level discourse prompts ▪ Designing critical thinking and problem-solving activities ▪ Varying level of complexity of activities and questions ▪ Formatively assessing students and adjusting instruction ▪ Designing multiple pathways to learn and demonstrate learning ▪ Conferencing with students ▪ Leveraging technology to promote student ownership	▪ Engaging in student-to-student discourse ▪ Authentically engaging in the lesson activities ▪ Working in collaborative groups ▪ Advocating for themselves and relevant learning outcomes ▪ Engaging in inquiry and formulating questions to drive learning ▪ Reflecting on learning ▪ Self-assessing learning and needs ▪ Appropriately using technology to enhance learning ▪ Creating learning activities ▪ Interpreting teacher and peer feedback
Personalized Learning	
▪ Embedding choice and opportunities for student input into learning activities and assessments ▪ Assessing student interests through *Getting to Know You Survey* or other means ▪ Structuring meaningful group tasks ▪ Varying questioning strategies and techniques ▪ Differentiating learning activities and assessments ▪ Providing individualized feedback ▪ Conferencing with students ▪ Providing instruction on how to think, solve problems, evaluate evidence, analyze arguments and generate hypotheses ▪ Leveraging technology to provide multiple opportunities for students to engage with the content	▪ Working on authentic challenge projects or real-world problems ▪ Working in groups and demonstrating meaningful collaboration ▪ Making decisions about their learning ▪ Generating questions and posing their own ▪ Proposing learning activities to support knowledge and skill acquisition ▪ Working on different activities and assignments ▪ Justifying and defending their thinking ▪ Influencing pace and path of learning ▪ Using technology to advance their learning ▪ Exploring areas of interest
Anytime, Anywhere Learning	
▪ Modeling online access to resources ▪ Reinforcing expectations for appropriate use of technology ▪ Including technology applications in lessons ▪ Providing real-world opportunities for students ▪ Challenging and rewarding student use of online tools ▪ Using technology to gather real-time data that formatively assesses and informs instruction ▪ Leveraging technology to provide and monitor anytime, anywhere access to content	▪ Using technology to work collaboratively with peers ▪ Exercising digital citizenship ▪ Using the appropriate technology during and beyond class period ▪ Following MPS technology expectations ▪ Directing their own learning outside of the classroom ▪ Accessing tools and information posted by the teacher ▪ Completing online assessments ▪ Bringing charged technology to class ▪ Selecting resources to further their own learning
Mastery-Based Learning (2018 -2019 implementation)	
▪ Providing and assessing students individually on clear learning targets ▪ Providing individualized feedback ▪ Advancing students through the curriculum ▪ Conferencing with students ▪ Monitoring individual and group progress ▪ Providing multiple opportunities for students to demonstrate mastery of content area standards	▪ Preparing for learning target assessments ▪ Initiating independent study ▪ Working on performance tasks ▪ Forming self-study groups ▪ Self-assessing ▪ Peer editing, feedback and review of assignments ▪ Sharing or presenting performance tasks ▪ Interpreting teacher and peer feedback and revising

This document is non-evaluative and should be used for self-reflection.

CORMIER   MERIDEN PUBLIC SCHOOLS
                                          Pride in All We Do

Figure 2.1b. Student-Centered Learning. This document was developed by Cormier Consulting, LLC in collaboration with the Meriden Public Schools

provide learning experiences to students that extend beyond the classroom walls. Through the use of digital tools, teachers and students are collaborating daily. Success was achieved and documented when one high school teacher shared, "I often found myself wishing there was a second teacher in the

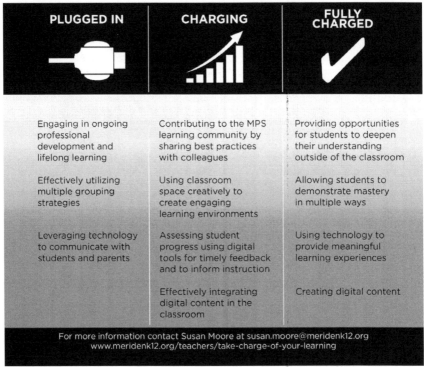

Figure 2.2. I'm Charged. Meriden Public Schools, Meriden, CT

classroom to support my students. Using technology, I realized the second teacher was me."

Why is it essential to embark on a digital transformation? Our students need us! We must guide and help them navigate their public school learning environment as they will likely be competing against their more affluent and advantaged peers across global markets. Today, optimal learning spaces must extend beyond traditional classroom walls, and students need to adapt and embrace the concept of lifelong learning.

- Key Takeaway: Our students are anxiously awaiting us to engage them and personalize their learning using technology.

HIRING THE RIGHT CHIEF TECHNOLOGY OFFICER

With technology taking center stage, it has never been more critical to ensure that school districts have the best Chief Technology Officer (CTO) in place. Your CTO will provide clarity to all stakeholders about the importance of your digital transformation. As an essential member of your team, your CTO should be aligned with your clear vision, guiding principles, and core values. When looking to hire your next CTO, consider the following four points:

COMMUNICATION MATTERS

Your CTO must communicate, collaborate, and create positive working relationships with teachers, administrators, support staff, and community stakeholders. Look for someone who has emotional intelligence and the ability to understand the desires and concerns of multiple stakeholders. Do not underestimate the need for someone who has compassion and can empathize with others. This person will be called on to build teams and distribute leadership.

TECHNOLOGY EXPERTISE ALONE IS NOT ENOUGH

Of course, this person needs to understand the technology side of the organization, but this position is more than wires, access points, and networks. Today's CTO must understand how technology connects to and supports the curriculum. How can technology resources support personalized student learning for all students? How can digital content engage students and allow teachers to provide direct instruction to small student groups? Does this person understand how technology is instrumental to daily instruction and that students and staff are stifled by network interruptions?

The CTO must be a teacher. While your CTO will not be your district's only technology teacher leader, your CTO will need to be a teacher at heart. Be less concerned with teaching credentials and certifications and more concerned with your CTO's ability to guide the learning process for a diverse group of staff in the educational institution. Whether modernizing maintenance, food services, transportation, or the classroom, your CTO's ability to ensure learning across all levels is critical. Teaching is about learning, growth, and development. Make sure your CTO understands and embraces this role.

LOOK FOR AN INNOVATION MINDSET

Your CTO will need a diverse skill set, and the job description will be complex and varied. Ultimately, your CTO will be called on to be a leader of change and an innovator of action. Hire someone who sees all the possibilities and can identify the "why." Avoid those so cautious that the fear of failure prevents them from ever realizing their own or the organization's full potential. Look for a visionary, a calculated risk-taker who sees change as an opportunity for progress—someone who is not looking for all the glory but rather to be a contributing member of a high-functioning team.

ELEVATE THE POSITION

If you find someone who can meet the first three conditions for success, you are a step ahead of others and ready to take your district to the next level. Elevate the position! Make sure your CTO is a key cabinet member involved in district direction and decisions. Allow your CTO the opportunity to present and share ideas with your administrators and the Board of Education. Lastly, listen to your CTO. Their skill set is unique, and their views are necessary.

Technology has forced us to look at teaching and learning through a new lens. We should look at hiring our CTO differently, as well. The speed of change has all of us working hard to keep up. More now than ever before, having the right CTO in place is essential to keep pace with your students and the ever-changing world in which we live. Hire the right CTO, and you will be on your way.

- Key Takeaway: Your Chief Technology Officer must be part of your core leadership team as they understand the role technology plays in advancing teaching and learning.

EXPANDING OPPORTUNITIES

Access to online content is essential for all students. Devices are an essential learning tool, and students should be allowed to keep them over the summer months. Many districts debated whether to collect all devices at the close of the school year out of fear too many would get lost, broken, or not returned. Those that took a chance discovered from the start that only a handful of devices were not returned, and devices that were broken could easily be repaired or replaced.

Districts also realized time savings by not having to collect and distribute devices. Meanwhile, permitting students to keep their devices over the summer opened up many opportunities, especially for students whose families did not always have additional devices at home. Also, students can sign out Wi-Fi hotspots if needed, enroll in online summer courses, or challenge themselves with district-supported digital content.

Gaming-rich environments are a place where our students feel comfortable and can experience success. But are our schools there yet? Some schools remain stuck in the past, thinking that gaming means the Oregon Trail but game-based learning has moved well beyond the trail. Gamification needs to play a crucial role in learning today because it engages learners, provides immediate feedback, and sets individual targets. Students can board a space shuttle, dive in our oceans, and backpack the Appalachian Mountains without leaving their classrooms. Progressive public schools are leveraging the benefits of virtual reality to level the playing field.

While we cannot create a road map for where technology will lead us, we must prepare students for careers that are still to be created. We also know one thing will not change, and that is that students who are better educated will have better opportunities. It will be today's students who are designing tomorrow's innovations. Our students have the fix; we need to stop and listen. Reimagine and reinvent your school system, and honor your students' voices and choices. Then your students will have expanded opportunities and make it happen for themselves, your schools, and your community.

- Key Takeaway: Help students expand their world with digital resources.

BLENDED LEARNING

Blended learning is commonplace today in K-12 education. However, making it effective takes planning and strategies to ensure that it is embraced by staff and effective for students. Begin small by laying the groundwork, evaluating your Wi-Fi, and implementing BYOD guidelines. Once these are in place, it is time to move toward a 1:1 environment with district-issued devices to use during the school year and summer months.

Create a buy-in. Teachers want to know that any new initiative will benefit their students and is not just another initiative that will be gone in a year. Make sure teachers embrace the change, see its usefulness, and are comfortable with what you are asking them to do. Ensure a smooth transition by establishing a team of technology-integration specialists and instructional coaches.

The technology-integration specialists can learn and test the new technology before asking teachers to integrate it into the curriculum. They can prepare for the common mistakes that staff might make and let them know that it is part of the learning process. Teachers are more secure using technology when they know they have technology specialists helping them plan lessons and, often, co-teach with them.

Provide choice for students. Offer a range of digital content programs that are embedded in must-do activities and can-do options. Students enjoy having a choice in their assignments which leads to greater student engagement and work completion. Students also appreciate opportunities to work independently, paired, or in small groups. In addition, students welcome immediate feedback and the gaming features that make learning fun!

Analyze digital content data to inform instruction. All digital platforms collect data on students' use of their programs. Monitor progress and modify instruction to meet student's individual needs by using key data points. Make connections early on between the teacher's effective use of the data and the necessity of engaging instruction. Changes made to the instructional process can be visible in your students' daily learning and their results on assessments.

Be clear and upfront with sharing the data collected. You want teachers to see their successes. By sharing this information openly, districts can show teachers when students are progressing at higher levels. Feedback from your staff at all levels is essential to student success. Identify what is working well and areas in need of improvement. Take on new challenges by replicating instructional success and being honest about failures. Schedule regular monthly meetings with building administrators and key teachers to focus on student and staff feedback and strategies needed to strengthen digital content usage and effectiveness.

Since blended learning can positively impact a district's overall success, many districts create a staff position dedicated to this work. This person's responsibility could be to analyze ways to maximize teacher use of the digital curriculum and provide assistance to staff as needed. The leader should work closely with teachers and technology-integration specialists and track and follow up on areas of concern. This position allows you to assess if the technology is user-friendly, supports instructional needs, and makes a difference in student learning and growth. Ultimately, this position can help districts determine if their investment is paying off.

Blended learning still requires both teachers and students to meet in face-to-face settings, but it provides students with some level of control over time, place, path, and pace. Teachers who truly value mastery over seat time embrace blended learning as a means of providing more individualized and personalized instruction for their students' exploration and learning. Students appreciate the flexibility in learning that is offered by a blended environment.

- Key Takeaway: Blended learning takes the best parts of traditional classroom instruction and pairs them with the best online educational materials.

DISTANCE LEARNING

Many districts were starting to engage in anytime, anywhere learning before the COVID-19 pandemic. With the abrupt closing of schools, districts with some technology experience utilized their devices and resources and pivoted to distance learning quickly. As schools reopen, components of distance learning will continue to have a place in the future of learning in all schools. When moving to a distance learning environment or providing a remote learning plan, staying true to your core values is essential.

In one district, students in Grades K-12 were provided with learning experiences that utilized digital content and core instruction from the teachers at each grade level. Synchronous learning combined with asynchronous learning provided students with a comprehensive learning experience. A single sign-on portal allows students to effectively access learning resources, whether on a home device or a district-issued device. Districts should also share the minimum number of minutes students need to access digital content as part of their weekly assignments.

Teachers in Grades K-2 provide lessons in Google Classroom. Students also complete 60 minutes of reading and math digital content daily. A weekly science lesson is also provided. Students in Grades 3–5 follow a similar format. Teachers post assignments in Google Classroom, and students complete learning activities at their level on their self-paced software programs. Students explore science concepts through gaming on various software programs.

Grade 6–8 students access Google Classrooms and complete activities in their specific digital content programs. Enable middle school students' emails so they can contact their teachers directly. At the high schools, teachers provide lessons in their content areas through Google Classroom. English and math teachers also monitor and support their students as they progress through reading and math digital content.

The district also recognized the importance of including Unified Arts in high-quality distance learning plans. Public schools need to provide opportunities for students to explore their passions, pursue their interests, and enjoy learning, whether operating in person or remotely. These activities are student-centered, engaging, and require minimal parental support. High school unified arts are credit-earning classes in a student's daily schedule. K-8 Unified Arts teachers also post weekly project-based learning assignments for remote learners. Students complete the work and teachers provide feedback and support.

Teachers and support staff collaborate, coordinate services, and communicate with families. Students access their general education curriculum and curriculum provided by the special education and related service staff through videos, platforms such as Google Classroom, 1:1 phone calls, and videoconferencing. Schools moving to a distance-learning option should create a distance learning plan, design memorandums of understanding with union partners and community partners, create job duties and schedules for all stakeholders, establish local distribution options, and communicate regularly with their families and stakeholders.

Stay true to your core values. Allow students to access assignments when convenient for them and their families. Encourage teachers to utilize multiple tools and strategies to connect with their students, whether online or in person. Your plan should provide all students with a vast array of learning experiences. Make sure your grade level teachers deliver effective core instruction and implement high-quality digital content and online resources. Create clear teacher expectations for distance learning in collaboration with your teachers and administrators' unions.

Provide personalized and adaptive content for all learners by focusing on sustaining weekly digital content requirements. Schools cannot ensure appropriate levels of home support or teacher capacity to provide distance learning successfully. Provide core curricular resources that your students, teachers, and families are familiar with using during a typical school day. With digital content in place and easily accessible, progressive districts are looking at expanding existing resources to challenge all learners.

Districts support their teachers, students, and parents by leveraging existing district resources. A help desk system with content coaches in place can support your students, families, and teachers. Provide tech tips via email, maintain a technology-integration website full of resources, and utilize Google Meets to support your teachers remotely. Tech support typically handled at the school level now needs to be accessible through a virtual format.

Allow families to complete an online form or call personnel for assistance. IT staff can usually troubleshoot the problem remotely. If not, families can pick up another device so students can complete assignments in a timely manner. Set clear teacher expectations. Teacher, student, and home expectations can be clearly outlined in a memorandum of understanding with your union partners.

Cloud-based professional development on digital tool usage and best practices for distance learning should be provided to all teachers and support staff. Coaches should be available to support teachers with digital content issues as well. Continue to support teachers remotely by providing them with easily accessible IT support. Virtual staff and online department meetings can be held to address any issues or concerns as they arise.

One of the keys to launching a distance learning plan is your ability to connect with parents through emails, phone calls, and texts. Districts sent thousands of messages to families throughout the first few weeks of school closure due to the pandemic. Administrators, teachers, and families needed to stay in close contact to support students during this transition period. Students in need of social-emotional learning skills, having difficulty engaging in distance learning, or requiring additional academics were supported virtually.

Whether a pandemic, parental pressure, student success, or resource allocation cause you to consider offering your students a distance learning option, know that it could be done well. There are seven keys for launching a high-quality distance learning program in your school or district:

- Set clear expectations that students, staff, and families understand. These expectations should include minimum participation minutes and usage guidelines.
- Insist that learning continues for your students and staff. Welcome the changes and realize that both students and staff will need to learn new skills, so be ready to support them.
- Let your staff be the experts! Teacher leaders, technology teachers, and department heads can offer online tutorial sessions to ensure successful implementation. Create a virtual help desk for parents and students in need of technical support.
- Go with what you know and what works. Vendors graciously offered free subscriptions and trials to districts during the pandemic. However, stick with what your people are already comfortable using. Embrace the programs and tools that your staff and students use every day. Add additional features from current digital partners before adding new tools, products, or vendors.
- Keep it simple. Students, parents, and staff are sorting through a high quantity of digital learning material in a rapidly changing environment. Limit the number of tools, as well as set district expectations that are clear and concise. Also, be committed to the long haul, as adjusting to change takes time.
- Be flexible, be ready to adapt, and do not expect to get it right on the first try. By planning, implementing, and monitoring what is working well, districts will adjust when difficulties arise.

- Do not let the chaos around us prevent us from stopping, recognizing, and celebrating the successes that are happening every day.

After months and months of distance learning and increased screen time, what support will our students need? The caseloads of social workers, psychologists, and support staff must be considered when building your distance program. Can we capitalize on the learnings of the pandemic and provide viable distance learning programs to support all our students? What are we doing to support our students socially, emotionally, and academically?

- Key Takeaway: Don't let the confines of a classroom stop the learning; learning can happen anywhere and anytime.

ADDRESSING THE FUTURE

As schools closed their doors for the school year and provided distance learning and virtual proms and graduations, thoughts moved to this school year and beyond. While politicians and municipal leaders scurried to realize savings from their Board of Education's school closure and distance learning implementation, educators looked to learn from their COVID-19 required digital transformation efforts. As health officials and economists predict future responses to the coronavirus disease, we must all begin preparing for the future of education, whether it occurred by natural occurrences or stakeholder desire.

As school districts across the nation closed out the worst unique school year in American public education's illustrious history, the planning for the unknown began. Communities—rural, suburban, urban, small, medium, and large—must ask themselves what will be the future of American public education? Will we leverage the learnings of the past year to think and act differently when it comes to what our schools can and should be?

Will students need more social-emotional support? How will we support students in our special education programs? How will we provide targeted interventions for our most vulnerable students? How will we assess and address learning gaps? What will be the future health and hygiene requirements? Will cocurricular and extracurricular activities exist? Will there be professional development, orientation, and parent conferences? What technology will be required to support all learners? And the most crucial question of all, what role will technology play in learning?

We know that school is much more than six hours a day, five days a week, and 180 days a year. Our students' learning takes place through varied cocurricular and extracurricular activities. Will our local performances occur in our auditoriums or through virtual performances? Will sports teams play an actual game with fans in the stands or sets of empty bleachers with online viewing options? Will eSports replace low enrollment teams? What about all the assemblies, field trips, clubs, and activities—will they happen? Will virtual tours rule the day?

None of us could have predicted a pandemic or planned for it, but most American public schools insisted that learning continued for their students. Students and staff have been flexible, supportive, and understanding. Today, public schools must look differently at the future of education and the role technology can play in leveling the playing field for all learners. In essence, this past year was the learning experiment that we needed to push the boundaries of public education in America. So what did we learn?

- No one will ever question the need to embrace technology in our schools.
- Devices and access are the new norms for all.
- All teachers, regardless of age, seniority, personal comfort, or grade level, can use technology to engage and personalize learning for their students.
- Keeping devices in neat device lockers at our schools or on classroom shelves is over. Get devices into the hands of students—all students, all ages, and all grade levels.
- School cancellations for snow, extreme heat, or facility issues should be over. Do not call a snow day—call a distance learning day.
- Digital content is here to stay.
- Parent notification and engagement are a must.
- Single sign-on is not a luxury—it is a necessity.

We also have learned from this experience several educational improvements that we can consider moving forward:

- Regionalization of teaching can occur across districts.
- Virtual Advanced Placement offerings allow enrollment of students across high schools.
- Distance learning is an alternative program for disengaged, disenfranchised, uncomfortable, or chronically absent students.
- Virtual Professional Development and Staff and Parent Conferences save time and increase participation.
- Increased collaboration among school districts, municipal departments, and nonprofit organizations can benefit our schools, staff, and students.

Public education in America has changed for the better. The pandemic has reignited educational imagination, supported technology integration, fostered innovation, and inspired all of us to become better educators and leaders. Accept the challenge of looking at education through an alternative lens. We have witnessed the powerful combination of teachers and technology coming together to support our students. These lessons will ensure that public schools will be ready to educate all learners regardless of what the future brings.

Hear the voices of your students and families, follow the guidance of health officials, and collaborate with teachers and staff. Let your students and staff health, safety, and well-being continue to guide your work and future planning. Insist on connectivity for all and purchase, repair, and replace student devices. Students and staff across our nation have shown us that quality distance learning programs can work for students and that technology can support student growth and staff development as well. Districts learned that they can keep students at the center when they personalize, differentiate, and engage.

Promote success and provide equitable learning opportunities for all students by embracing digital learning. Districts will recognize budget efficiencies and improve student outcomes when they embrace technology in operational systems and student learning. A catalyst for change is the collaborative culture that can be fostered in your schools. Students are leading the charge and making believers out of their communities. Instructional leaders are ready for change, teachers are dedicated and committed to innovation, and boards and unions are incredibly supportive and prepared to be change agents.

While efforts to support funding increases remain part of educational leaders' jobs, creating significant efficiencies by embracing technology can help all leaders utilize their funds more effectively. Prepare your students for college and career success, realize budget savings, and create appropriate, challenging learning environments for your students by insisting that technology is a key component of your district's improvement plan.

We believe public education can be a great equalizer if we unleash the potential of our students, staff, and families. By leveraging technology for learning, we can prepare diverse student populations for lifelong success. Technology and the use of high-quality digital content has a proven track record of engaging and advancing student learning. Districts need to be prepared to take on this challenge and learn from others what pitfalls to avoid.

All school districts are dealing with unstable resources, increased accountability, and more significant student needs. We have watched districts launch campaigns to save their schools, organize support for our school rallies, and march on city hall. Other districts are turning to technology for answers. Facing COVID-19, racial unrest, increasing special education costs, teacher evaluations, and Common Core State Standards implementation costs, and the tasks ahead became even more disconcerting.

Central office teams can hold budgeting forums to discuss keeping students at the center of all decisions. Planning can include discussions around the following themes:

- Repurpose resources
- Drop what's not working
- Manage budget cost drivers
- Secure private funding
- Build community support and partnership
- Invest in staff

These can become your guiding principles as you prepare for the future. And preparing for the future means that technology will continue to play a critical role in your educational institution. Technology integration can improve student and staff learning and provide opportunities for operational efficiencies. Support technology-based blended learning by collapsing academic levels to ensure rigorous coursework for all, change mindsets to value effort, implement mastery-based grading practices, and give all students greater access to high-level classes.

Improving learning outcomes for your students requires students to be put at the center of all schooling decisions. Collaborate and empower them, encourage technology use, give them voice and choice in their learning and expose them to real-world learning experiences. To prepare your stakeholders for the technology shift in your district and gain community support, share device savings and launch a campaign that floods your community with data and information through student-led forums and workshops.

Student engagement will spike as students are given a greater voice and an opportunity to share their work. Develop parent, staff, and student surveys to hear their concerns and answer questions from all stakeholders. Buy-in can help you introduce technology as a learning tool and address concerns and, sometimes, misconceptions. Eliminating all potential technology transformation pitfalls will allow you to keep the focus on technology-enhanced student learning.

To continue supporting and improving student learning as a district, invest in online resources and applications to accommodate individual learning needs. To provide students with daily access to these programs, make operational changes which include reallocating and reusing resources. Functional changes that support technology integration should include structural space modifications, automation of systems, and utilization of community partners.

Look at the floor plans of your schools and identify large multiuse spaces that could support your district's transformation through creative facility usage and innovative staffing. Redesign your media centers to enhance student-centered learning and support blended-learning instructional approaches. These adaptive learning spaces can engage large numbers of students with minimal professional staff supervision. These spaces should provide flexibility and allow for collaborative student-centered learning.

Having a critical central office leader who understands curriculum and technology should be the first step in investing in our staff. This role can be beneficial as your district begins a complete overhaul and automation of systems. Online applications, online vacation requests, automated work orders, automated cafeteria operations, online out-of-district placements, automated transportation systems, family-school liaison tracking tools, and online substitute teaching assignments all should be part of your system's automation efforts.

The online substitute system process can be brought back in-house and the online solution implemented, thus realizing significant savings through automation of substitute teacher operations. Substantial time savings can be realized through the automation of food service. Food service staff spends hours processing numerous annual Free and Reduced Lunch Applications. Considerable cost savings can also be realized through the automation of energy management systems. Controlling heating, air-conditioning, and lighting from a central application provides management oversight from one location, under the supervision of central office personnel.

The district should incorporate interactive websites where all stakeholders can easily access documents and resources. Paperless board meetings and flyers should be available electronically. Price points on Chromebooks are allowing many districts to go 1:1 cost-effectively. To support your transition to student-centered learning environments and realize budget savings, media and classroom reading selections can be purchased in digital format.

Improve efficiency and save valuable resources by launching your own digital transformation. Utilizing best practices can ensure a smooth transition to blended learning, authentic use of devices, and increased student learning. Technology is here to stay! Your students and staff are embracing the challenge and enhancing the learning. The community is recognizing the impact of technology in their lives.

- Key Takeaway: The power of connecting teachers and technology will challenge how we think about education and how we will support all of our learners.

DISCUSSION PROMPTS

What role does technology play in your district? Classrooms? Operations? Services?

How do you solicit school and community support for your digital transformation efforts?

How has technology improved learning for students?

What supports do your digital content partners provide to students and staff?

How can technology impact the future direction of education?

Chapter 3

Embracing the Whole Child and Advancing Equity

Chloe had just spent her lunch period eating alone once again. As the bell rang for dismissal time, Chloe threw away her apple and returned to Period 6. Students took out their Chromebooks to complete the district's annual Fall Student Climate Survey. Chloe, who was frustrated with the start of her school year, eagerly began answering the questions. The school psychologist made it a point to be in the hallway as she left class, and later in the day, casually stopped to speak with Chloe about her day.

Chloe didn't know that the principal and school psychologists had received a trigger email from the Student Climate Survey alerting them that a student could be in crisis. Chloe had written that her classmates were bullying her, and she had no one to talk to about it. Then, together, the team made a plan for Chloe to support her in developing positive relationships with her classmates and turned around a rough start to the school year.

CLIMATE SUITE ASSESSMENTS

If public schools are going to be the great equalizer, they need to provide more than just academics for students. Great schools make an effort to get to know their students, their interests, and how their home life may be affecting their learning in school. Addressing the social-emotional needs of students can positively impact the student's day and their overall school success. While many teachers can assess their students' emotional states when they enter the classroom, tools that dig deeper can provide a wealth of information.

Implementing school and climate measures can help identify the academic and emotional needs of students. Teachers and support staff can work with students to develop grit, perseverance, a growth mindset, motivation, and respect for others. Our public schools cannot ignore the social-emotional

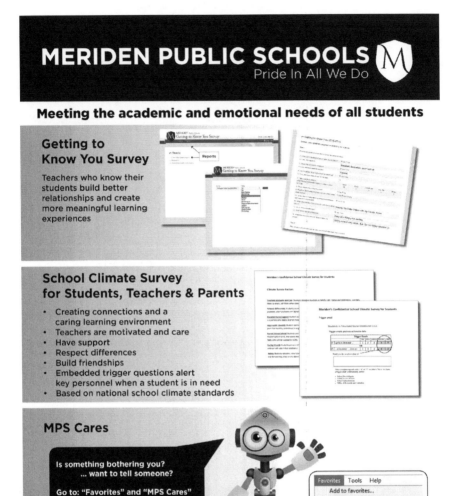

Figure 3.1a.

needs of students. Socially emotionally at-risk students frequently become disengaged, stay home or skip classes, and sometimes drop out of school. They often lose their motivation to attend school or work to their full potential.

Public schools need to identify "at-risk" students early and intervene quickly to ensure all students have the emotional support they need to succeed. Meriden Public Schools' Office of Research and Evaluation has

MERIDEN PUBLIC SCHOOLS Ⓜ
Pride In All We Do

Meeting the academic and emotional needs of all students

In Meriden, we are embracing a student-centered approach in both academics and social-emotional supports, such as fostering the psychological constructs of perseverance, positive mindset, engagement, motivation, caring, and respect for others. Social-emotional at-risk students become disengaged, skip class and sometimes drop out of school. They lose their intrinsic motivation to attend school or do a good job. In Meriden, we are beginning to identify these "at-risk" students early and intervene swiftly. We have developed three instruments that help us promote student social-emotional health and positive teacher-student relationships: Getting to Know You Survey; Meriden's School Climate Survey; and MPS Cares.

Getting to Know You Survey
The primary purpose of the Getting to Know You Survey is to help foster positive teacher-student relationships. Based on national motivation research, questions concerning student expectations of improving this year and what they do when schoolwork gets hard — this positive mindset is an important factor of improving the survey. Students are asked how hard they worked last year and the personal value of each subject to them. These data allow us to measure, monitor and foster student motivation by subject area and discover the types of instructional practices that work best for our students. Students are also asked about outside interests such as sports, music, art and reading. This information helps teachers build positive relationships with their students, as well as guide student-centered reading tasks and personalized assignments. Teachers have access to only their own student information and the data can be subject specific. This online survey is administered to students in grades 4 to 12 and new students who arrive during the school year.

School Climate Survey
The Meriden School Climate Survey provides valid measures of school climate and generates actionable data that identify students who are experiencing a social-emotional problem, such as not feeling valued or social isolation. Meriden's online survey is confidential, developmentally sensitive and has been published in academic journals. Students are informed their answers will not be shared with anyone, unless someone is going to be harmed. Three of the items ask students if they have been hit or threatened, if mean rumors are being spread about them, and if they have a friend they can trust. Depending upon each student's response, the customized software immediately sends a trigger email to school psychologists, social workers and administration for immediate social-emotional support. Survey factors include: Teachers Care; Safety; Respect Differences; Caring Friends and Aggression. The survey is administered to grades 3-12 in the fall and spring each school year.

MPS Cares
Some students face new social-emotional problems and need to talk to someone. MPS Cares is a student-initiated, online supplement to our student climate survey and available throughout the school year. Students share if they have a problem with friends or if people are mean to them. If a student answers "yes" to either of these questions, a trigger email is automatically sent to school counselors and support is moments away.

IMPROVED SCHOOL CLIMATE		
Suspensions	↓86%	✔+
Expulsions	↓95%	✔+
Arrests	↓96%	✔+
REDUCTIONS SINCE 2010-2011		

For more information Contact
Dr. Al Larson at 203.630.4122
al.larson@meridenk12.org • www.meridenk12.org

Figure 3.1b. School Climate Survey. Meriden Public Schools, Meriden, CT

developed an online Climate Suite of four instruments to help promote student social-emotional health and positive teacher-student relationships. This Climate Suite consists of a School Climate Survey, Getting to Know You Survey, MPS Cares, and Transitional Essays.

MERIDEN PUBLIC SCHOOLS

Here, Students Succeed

Getting to Know You Survey

"Today, I want you to think about next school year and your new teachers. Your new teachers want to know about you. Meriden's Getting to Know You survey allows you to tell them what you like and what you don't like, as well as your interests and something about you. This will help get next year off to a great start! This survey is important. Tell your next year's teachers about you."

Part I - First, tell us something about what you like to do outside of school.

1. Is there a particular sport you are good at, or you enjoy?
2. What sport?
3. Do you play a musical instrument?
4. If yes, what instrument do you play?
5. If no, would you like to learn a musical instrument?
6. If yes, what type of instrument do you want to learn?
7. I attend religious services (church, synagogue/temple/mosque, or another house of worship). 8. Do you sing in a choir or like to sing?
9. Would you like to sing in a group at school or learn more about singing?
10. What other activities do you enjoy doing either in or out of school?
11. Do you have a favorite book?
12. If yes, what is the title of this book?
13. What else would you like us to know about you as a person?

Part II - This next group of questions deals with how you generally feel about school subjects. We use your answers to help improve our schools.

Likert Scale: 1 Never 2 Rarely 3 Sometimes 4 Very Often 5 Always

1. During this past school year, the classroom activities in my math class were really meaningful to me.
2. During this past school year, the classroom activities in my Language Arts (ILA) reading class were really meaningful to me.
3. During this past school year, the classroom activities in my science class were really meaningful to me.
4. During this past school year, the classroom activities in my social studies (history) class were really meaningful to me.

Figure 3.2a.

SCHOOL CLIMATE SURVEY

The School Climate Survey has an embedded automatic trigger email sent to the principal, school psychologist, social worker, and other appropriate personnel if a student reports a problem or appears to be in crisis. Administered to Grades 3–12 annually in the fall and spring, the School Climate Survey identifies students who may be dealing with social-emotional challenges, such as being bullied or not having any friends. Students are informed their

5. During this past school year, the classroom activities in my physical education (gym) class were really meaningful to me.

    Likert Scale: 1 Really Dislike   2 Dislike It   3 It's Okay   4 Like It   5 Really Like It

6. During this past school year, how much did you like math class?
7. During this past school year, how much did you like Language Arts (ILA) reading?
8. During this past school year, how much did you like social studies class?
9. During this past school year, how much did you like science class?
10. During this past school year, how much did you like physical education (gym) class?

    Likert Scale: 1 Not At All   2 A Little   3 More or Less 4 Hard   5 Very Hard

11. During this past school year, how hard did you work in math class?
12. During this past school year, how hard did you work in social studies (history) class?
13. During this past school year, how hard did you work in science class?
14. During this past school year, how hard did you work in physical education (gym) class?
15. Last year, how much effort did you put into your Language Arts (ILA) class?

Part III - This next group of questions deals with your interests and you as a person. Carefully answer each question. Your answers are very important.
Likert Scale: 1 Strongly Disagree 2 Disagree 3 Sometimes   4 Agree   5 Strongly Agree

1. Even with a difficult task, I keep trying and don't give up.
2. One reason I go to school is because I enjoy learning about my favorite subjects.
3. During this past school year, when math got hard, someone (teachers or others) helped me.
4. I am a very good reader.
5. I am good at physical education (gym) activities.
6. My schoolwork gives me a sense of accomplishment.
7. If something is important to me, I'll keep working to get to it, no matter how hard it may be.
8. One reason I go to school is because learning new things gives me a sense of satisfaction

Figure 3.2b.

answers will remain anonymous unless someone is going to be harmed or is in danger.

GETTING TO KNOW YOU SURVEY

The purpose of the Getting to Know You Survey is to help teachers get to know their incoming students better and develop positive relationships with

MERIDEN PUBLIC SCHOOLS M

Here, Students Succeed

9. For me, it is important to eat a healthy diet.
10. During this past school year, when reading got hard, someone (teachers or others) helped me.
11. Socially, I fit in at school.
12. It is important that I know about social studies and history.
13. I am determined to learn even the most difficult schoolwork.
14. I feel that I can be myself at school.
15. During this past school year, when social studies (history) got hard, someone (teachers or others) helped me.
16. For me, it is important to be able to read well.
17. I feel free to express my ideas and opinions at school.
18. For me, it is important to do math well.
19. If I'm not good at something, I stop trying.
20. In school, I work well with all my classmates.
21. During this past school year, when science got hard, someone (teachers or others) helped me.
22. I get a satisfied feeling in finding out about new things.
23. This past school year, homework was either just too hard or I didn't have time to do it.
24. It is important that I know about science.
25. If possible, I really want to go to some college after high school.
26. I find what we study at school interesting.
27. I am physically fit.
28. I give up when schoolwork starts getting too difficult.
29. I am really good at math.
30. It doesn't matter how hard you work in school; it has a lot to do with luck.
31. I am really good at science.
32. It's OK to make mistakes in class, as long as you're learning.
33. It is important to exercise on a regular basis.
34. If a person works harder, he/she can do better.
35. I am very good at social sciences (history).
36. I do as little studying as possible; extra studying is not worth it.
37. Getting something wrong makes me want to understand why and do better next time.
38. When classwork gets hard, I just work harder.

Figure 3.2c.

them. The survey was developed with input from students and staff and asks questions about growth mindset, expectations for the upcoming school year, and how students feel about the subjects they are taking. Students are also asked about their outside interests, such as music, art, and sports.

All this information helps a teacher not only build positive relationships but increase student motivation. For example, a student may not be enjoying reading, but if a teacher knows that the student is interested in music, then she can find biographies about famous musicians for the student to read, which

MERIDEN PUBLIC SCHOOLS
Here, Students Succeed

Part IV - This last group of questions deals with your diet and exercise. We use this information to improve physical education and our lunch programs.

Likert Scale: 1 0 days/week 2 1-2 days/week 3 3-4 days/week 4 5-6 days/week 5 everyday

1. I usually drink 3 or more bottles/glasses (36 ounces or more) of unflavored water.
2. I usually eat fruits and/or vegetables.
3. Usually, I am physically active (run, swim, exercise, play sports) for 30 minutes or more.
4. What do you want to do after high school?

Classroom teachers are asked to preview their future classes in August, <u>before the start of school</u> in order to see which students are most at-risk and disengaging from their subject. The customized Getting to Know You software color codes a student's score to highlight which students will need extra care and consideration (which students feel they are not capable and doomed to do poorly).

Figure 3.2d. Getting to Know You Survey. Meriden Public Schools, Meriden, CT

could pique greater reading interest. Similarly, if a student expresses an interest in sports, a teacher can get the student interested in reading by introducing sports magazines or stories about football and baseball.

The survey is administered to students in Grades 4–12 early in the school year and new students when they arrive and enter school during the school year. Teachers can access the data for their classes or individual students. By administering the survey early in the school year, teachers get a jumpstart on getting to know their students. We know that it's all about building trusting relationships!

MPS CARES

If students want help or need someone to talk to, they can complete the online Meriden Public Schools' tool MPS Cares, available throughout the school year. Posters are displayed in hallways throughout the school, encouraging students to ask for help. When a student completes this tool, a trigger email is automatically sent to a school counselor who immediately seeks out the student to offer support.

TRANSITION ESSAYS

Transitioning to a large high school can be stressful for many students. Transition Essays are a tool designed to help students realize that others have faced similar issues in high school, which they resolved successfully. To develop the transition essays, students wrote about some of the difficulties they encountered in their transition to or during high school, how these problems had improved, and what factors had proven most helpful. Students select a challenge they are facing from about 100 online essays which illustrate different scenarios.

Many Grade 9 students are apprehensive about their ninth grade year. To help them transition smoothly, students complete Grade 9 Transition Writing Assignments. Seniors wrote essays about their experiences adjusting to high school. By reading about others' experiences and responding in turn, ninth grade students gained more confidence and became more comfortable in high school.

SAFETY MANAGEMENT SUPPORT

Partnerships with safety management companies prove to be essential in both in-person learning and distance learning. When a district receives a notification from the vendor, support staff can contact the families and include emergency personnel if needed. Safety Management also helps create positive school climates and teaches students how to become responsible digital citizens.

- Key Takeaway: Climate Suite tools support students, help teachers know their students better and encourage positive teacher-student relationships.

DEVELOPING A DISTRICT-WIDE
SOCIAL-EMOTIONAL LEARNING PROGRAM

Educators must help students build social-emotional learning skills to navigate the challenges of school and society. This becomes even more critical in communities where a large percentage of students receive free and reduced-price meals, and the impact of poverty was visible prior, during, and now as we continue to navigate the pandemic and the challenges that lie ahead. The best way to meet the needs of the whole child is to start early so you can minimize the number of disengaged and disenfranchised students in the upper grades. In response, districts need to create district-wide social-emotional learning (SEL) programs.

To address these needs, our district quickly pulled together a team of teachers at each school over the summer to review programs that were currently in place and develop a consistent plan. In addition, the team worked with a Board Certified Behavior Analyst to implement a uniform approach across grade levels. The team helped develop resources and sample lessons for teachers to use during the year.

Elementary teachers now start each day with 20 minutes of SEL instruction. All students are presented with the same concepts at their instructional level. The district's SEL Roadmap provides topics such as compassion, empathy, and respect that become the lesson's focus. Flexibility is built into the daily schedule so that teachers can maximize teachable moments throughout the school day. Literature focused on social-emotional learning was incorporated into every classroom. Monthly, teachers receive professional development focused on upcoming topics and implementation strategies.

Secondary school teachers support students during their weekly advisory meetings. During this time, topics include college and career readiness, student success plans, and social-emotional learning strategies. With students in greater need of social-emotional support, the district began to look for SEL materials. Again, a team of teachers reviewed numerous resources and developed a plan to be implemented at the secondary schools.

- Key Takeaway: Social-emotional learning should be embedded across all grade levels and for all students.

EQUITY AND ACCESS

Public school districts continue to be proactive in combating systemic racism in their schools. They embrace the richness of their diversity, value their tapestry of different colors and cultures, and remain committed to addressing discrimination and unconscious bias. To ensure that all students have access to high-quality educational experiences and graduate college, career, and life ready, all districts should apply an equity lens to their work. Our district's long-standing commitment to equity is evident in initiatives implemented during the last decade.

Our district eliminated tracking and ensured courses were rigorous and at a college level. It implemented "no zero" grading practices to support students and transitioned from traditional to student-centered learning classes. We opened access to all courses, including honors, Advanced Placement, and Early College Experience. Restorative practices and youth dialogues sessions were initiated. Resources were reallocated to provide a 1:1 environment with district-issued Chromebooks, and mobile hotspots for families needing internet access. Also, students were allowed to keep their Chromebooks over the summer to access online learning.

With these initiatives in place, the next step was to provide racial equity training to staff by developing a cadre of Equity Leaders who were teachers who showed an interest and commitment to this work. This critical work is best accomplished when colleagues are available on a timely basis and engage other staff members in meaningful conversations about culturally responsive classrooms and unconscious and conscious bias in their relationships with each other and their students.

Districts should develop an equity statement. It can be posted on district websites and shared at different venues, including convocation, board meetings, administrators' meetings, faculty meetings, and parent open houses. Brochures, flyers, and presentations to organizations, such as the Rotary Club and the Chamber of Commerce, are other community outreach methods that may garner community support. District statements on advancing equity are best developed with input from all stakeholders and re-examined and expanded as you reflect upon your experiences.

Our public school district's equity statement is as follows:

> To achieve equity and access for all, we must collectively challenge existing inequities, build meaningful relationships, and actively remove barriers to success. We value the uniqueness and varied experiences of all our students and staff. Regardless of racial identity, sexual orientation and gender identity, socioeconomic status, or prior learning experiences, all students must have access to equitable learning opportunities and digital resources to expand their world. The recognition of unconscious or conscious systemic and individual bias continues to guide our efforts and commitment to assure equity and high-quality education for all.

EQUITY LEADERS AND RACIAL
AWARENESS TRAINING MODULES

The district sought out funding from a foundation that allowed us to embark upon a two-year process to train 12 Equity Leaders with five at each of our two high schools, one representing elementary schools and one representing middle schools. A consultant worked with the Equity Leaders during release days and after school developing their awareness of racial equity. Once Equity Leaders were comfortable and knowledgeable in this area, the consultant engaged the group in creating racial equity training modules for all staff. The modules were designed around guiding questions which became the primary drivers.

DEFINING RACIAL EQUITY

Racial Equity Series Overview

SESSION	TITLE	GUIDING QUESTIONS	OBJECTIVES	AGENDA
1	**Defining Racial Equity**	*What is racial equity? Why is it important to have a shared and common understanding of key terms related to racial equity? What makes this work difficult or uncomfortable? Why is it important to address racial equity in our schools?*	▪ Engage in personal reflection and demonstrate an openness to learn & grow; ▪ Develop shared meaning of key terms related to racial equity; ▪ Understand the impact of race/racism on our practice as educators; and ▪ Increase levels of racial consciousness.	1. Introduction: Session Outcomes, Purpose/Non-Purpose, Norms, Considerations, & Warm-up 2. The R-Word 3. Defining Equity & Other Key Terms 4. Moving Forward... Why Address Racial Equity in Schools?
2	**Increasing Our Racial Consciousness**	*Why race? What is our data telling us? How racially conscious are we? What makes this work difficult or uncomfortable? Why is it important to address racial equity in our schools?*	▪ Engage in personal reflection and demonstrate an openness to learn & grow; ▪ Understand the impact of race/racism on our practice as educators; and ▪ Increase levels of racial consciousness.	1. Introduction: Session Outcomes, Review of: Purpose/Non-Purpose, Norms and Session Warm-up 2. Why Race? How Does Racism Exist in Our Society & in Our Schools? 3. Increasing Racial Consciousness 4. Moving Forward... Finding A Balance
3	**Engaging in Difficult Conversations**	*How can difficult conversations lead to growth and improvement? What tools can we use to sustain conversations and understand differing perspectives? How can we better understand defensiveness and denial (ours and others)?*	▪ Engage in personal reflection and demonstrate an openness to learn & grow; ▪ Learn & practice tools for engaging in difficult conversations; ▪ Understand the impact of race/racism on our practice as educators; and ▪ Increase levels of racial consciousness.	1. Introduction: Session Outcomes, Purpose/Non-Purpose, Norms, Considerations, & Warm-up 2. Difficult Conversations: *The Challenge, The Zone, & Common Responses* 3. Tools to Support Difficult Conversations, Reflection, & Growth 4. Applying the Tools

Figure 3.3a.

SESSION	TITLE	GUIDING QUESTIONS	OBJECTIVES	AGENDA
4	*The Impact of Microaggressions & Unconscious Bias*	*In what ways do microaggressions and unconscious biases impact our students of color?* *How can we increase our level of awareness or racial consciousness?* *How might microaggressions and unconscious biases affect racial identity and stereotype threat?*	▪ Engage in personal reflection and demonstrate an openness to learn & grow; ▪ Develop a deeper understanding of the impact microaggressions and unconscious biases have on our students; and ▪ Increase levels of racial consciousness and awareness.	1. Introduction & Warm-Up: Session Outcomes, Purpose/Non-Purpose, Norms, & Considerations 2. The Messages We Send: *Unconscious Bias & Microaggressions* 3. Intention vs Impact 4. Case Study 5. Next Steps

Figure 3.3b. Racial Equity Series Overview. This document was developed by Cormier Consulting, LLC in collaboration with the Meriden Public Schools

DEFINING RACIAL EQUITY

What is racial equity? How can you develop a shared and common understanding of key terms related to racial equity? What makes this work difficult or uncomfortable? Why is it important to address racial equity in our schools?

INCREASING OUR RACIAL CONSCIOUSNESS

Why race? What is our data telling us? How racially conscious are we? What makes this work difficult or uncomfortable? Why is it important to address racial equity in our schools?

ENGAGING IN DIFFICULT CONVERSATIONS

How can difficult conversations lead to growth and improvement? What tools can we use to sustain conversations and understand differing perspectives? How can we better understand defensiveness and denial (ours and others)?

THE IMPACT OF MICROAGGRESSIONS AND UNCONSCIOUS BIAS

In what ways do microaggressions and unconscious biases impact our students of color? How can districts' stakeholders increase post-graduation awareness or racial consciousness? How might microaggressions and unconscious biases affect racial identity and stereotype threat?

These modules were turn keyed with Equity Leaders presenting them to high school staff during early release days and contracted professional learning days. With a high school staff of about a hundred educators at each school, Equity Leaders were paired into six teams which facilitated smaller groups of under 20 educators to ensure interactive and meaningful conversations. After each presentation, the Equity Leaders would debrief with the consultant, who provided feedback and advice on handling difficult conversations.

As the Equity Leaders gained confidence and expertise, they organized after school book clubs and other events at their schools. Soon, middle and elementary school teachers were requesting racial equity awareness training. The consultant provided racial awareness workshops to all middle and elementary school teachers during contracted professional learning opportunities days, followed up by Equity Leaders presenting a more in-depth series of workshops after school for interested teachers.

As an outgrowth of these efforts, a District Sub-Committee offered a summer book club to administrators and developed equity teams at each elementary school. In addition, Equity Leaders continue to present components of racial equity awareness training modules at Board of Education meetings, Administrators' Meetings, Elementary and Secondary Principals' Meetings, and Administrators' Retreats. An outgrowth of the effectiveness of the high school Equity Leaders initiative was hiring a central office person dedicated to equity to bring the work to the elementary and middle schools. The next phase of the work will also include professional learning relating to sexual orientation and gender identity.

AFFINITY GROUPS

Personnel directors across the country are working hard to recruit and maintain teachers of color in their communities. To provide ongoing support to colleagues, many districts have started to create Affinity Groups where teachers of color and other interested teachers meet together to discuss mutual concerns, school topics, and provide ongoing support to one another. Affinity Groups often span more than one district, present to other educators interested in starting an Affinity Group within their district, and encourage their members to accompany personnel directors to help recruit teachers of color at local, state, and regional recruitment fairs.

Effective practices from districts promoting equitable opportunities are as follows:

- No-Cost Equity Components
- Review Board of Education policies
- Remove lower-level classes
- Initiate no-zero grading procedures
- Support Bring Your Own Device (BYOD) guidelines
- Reallocate funds for mobile devices
- Develop career pathways
- Create academic and emotional supports
- Provide open access to all high-level classes
- Implement classes for college credit
- Offer virtual college tours
- Present college readiness seminars
- Celebrate the success of students

Administrators, teachers, parents, and community volunteers supporting these activities can make a difference. These team members are enthusiastic about the initiatives because they understand the mission, support the efforts, and realize public education's significance and value to the success of our children. If Boards establish a clear vision, put students at the center, involve unions in the planning, and ensure that families and staff work together, all students will succeed. We cannot turn back on the past or repeat the past—our students, families, staff, and stakeholders depend on us.

- Key Takeaway: Equitable opportunities and access for all require a comprehensive approach and support from multiple stakeholders.

After a decade of dispensing out-of-school suspensions to the same angry, disenfranchised, or ambivalent students and their disappointed, tired, or bewildered parents, one district realized that there had to be a better way to handle discipline problems. Schools cannot teach students if they are not in school. Moreover, recent studies document that students who feel connected to school are likely to improve accountability measures. To achieve success, students need to have a sense of belonging and attachment.

Unfortunately, suspensions disconnect students who are already experiencing difficulties by further alienating them. Yet, administrators have used out-of-school suspensions for students with chronic tardiness, truancy, and minor behavior infractions for years. Recent legislation passed by various state general assemblies and signed into law requires in-school suspension except when students pose a danger to persons or property or serious disruption to the educational process.

These new laws have districts searching for creative alternatives to unproductive out-of-school suspensions. An In-School Suspension Program is an alternative that can meet the academic and behavioral needs of students, staff, and families. This type of program can provide a safe, supervised suspension program separate from the regular school environment while still focused on academics and student learning.

SEPARATE BUT EQUAL

Another district separates students with demonstrated behavior issues from their peers but maintains students' connectedness with school officials, teachers, and current school work. They also provide a quiet classroom that permits and documents school assignment completion and submission. Teachers also commit to providing current assignments and present students with daily school work assignments. In addition to reviewing the rules and completing school assignments, students complete a personal narrative and participate in exercises meant to strengthen their self-respect, responsibility, and readiness to learn.

This district created an accountability action plan that asks students to reflect on their behavior, the ensuing consequences, alternate decision options, and possible remediation strategies. Students answer the following questions: Why is school important? How could school be better for you? Do you have a post-graduation plan? The respect, responsibility, and readiness to learn assignments encourage students to identify positive behavior patterns and link them to decision-making scenarios.

The focus of quality alternative programs needs to be discipline, not punishment. Components should address the root cause of the behavior issue. Why was the student suspended? What actions were carried out, and what consequences were issued? This time should be used to strengthen academic skills. More positive results can be generated by providing students an opportunity to reflect on their behavior or alternative decision-making choices. Facilitate discussions related to specific offenses and consistently link positive student values to resulting student decisions and actions. Be sure to define the benefits of self-regulation.

The Accountability Action Plan is the final step in encouraging students to become responsible for their behavior and make better decisions. Develop the plan with the students and make sure they have input. Assess the need for an apology and a timely response. What do they need to change? How will things be different? Finally, follow up with students to ensure that they are using new strategies and prosocial skills.

Too often, students with behavioral problems are prematurely assigned to special education for evaluations and potential placement. Rather, program supervisors should spend time getting to know their students and become an additional resource in positive preventative measures. Develop an Early Intervention Core Team that explores individual students' educational options before considering a referral to special education programs. Administrative staff, counselors, social workers, resource officers, and teaching staff need to work closely to support the student.

While serving an in-school suspension, students complete the teacher-provided assignments that they would be missing with the support of a caring staff member. Completed work is submitted electronically to the teacher. This timely and positive feedback allows students to revise work and keep up with their class. In addition, being prepared and on track will enable students to return to class with greater confidence.

When searching for staff to support these students, look for someone creative, confident, and genuinely interested in student success. Today's staff must connect with students, assist students with school work, work well with teachers, and be prepared to contribute to the broader school community. The individual's respect for students must be demonstrated and based on the belief that all students can be academically and behaviorally successful.

Students leave in-school suspension with increased awareness and some new behavior management tools. For example, one student wrote in his accountability action plan: "After a long day in my in-school suspension, I have learned to deal more positively with similar situations in the future." In addition, students learn to realize that their negative patterns are getting in the way of their own goals. Students should feel bad about their behavior but not about who they are as a person.

Often, outsiders ask if a day of in-school suspension can make a difference? The in-school suspension provides students with a structured program and a caring staff member. As a result, the opportunity to change behaviors and form relationships that positively impact a student's academics is possible. Out-of-school suspension, other than for severe infractions, isolates students and causes them to fall further behind in their work. Effective in-school suspension should help to reduce the school dropout rate, decrease discipline referrals, and minimize out-of-school suspensions.

- Key Takeaway: Develop in-school suspension programs that support, not punish, students.

RESTORATIVE PRACTICES

Districts looking for an option aside from in-school or out-of-school suspensions, that are non-punitive and promote positive relationships, found that restorative practices address that need. The implementation of these practices builds relationships and develops collaborative classroom communities. Restorative practices encourage conversations between teachers and students as well as between students.

All the people affected by the negative behavior or incident meet to talk about how it made them feel and how to rectify this situation in the classroom. Often districts start this program by enlisting the help of a restorative practices consultant to provide professional learning for staff members. The most successful programs have staff support but are truly student-led.

One district created a District Culture and Climate Committee, which formulated an implementation plan for a series of secondary school training over two years and then followed that up by training at the elementary level. The skills of restorative practices involve being nonjudgmental, mindful of others, honest, respectful, and a probing questioner. Also, restorative practices help to reduce school violence and bullying. They also provide effective leadership to restore relationships and repair harm between individuals.

Gradually, as your teachers become more empathetic and comfortable using restorative practices for more serious behaviors, they can begin using either reactive or proactive restorative practices in their own classrooms. As administrators and teachers become better skilled with the process, they can develop school committees to begin using restorative practices when working with suspended and expelled students. It is not an easy road to accept new ways of dealing with behavioral and emotional issues, but progress is being made in our public schools. Again, it's all about relationships!

- Key Takeaway: Punitive discipline never solves the problem; look for other avenues to support positive behaviors.

STAYING FUELED UP

Many districts are exploring universal free breakfast and lunch programs for all students as they recognize that students cannot learn if they are hungry. Just as schools ensure that students have technology and textbooks, they must insist that they have a healthy breakfast and lunch. Elementary and middle school students can have breakfast in their classrooms while high school students can participate in successful grab-and-go models.

Food and Nutrition Services Programs often operate in isolation from the district's school system. Private providers and separate entities set the costs of meals and leave districts with limited oversight and involvement. Progressive districts can change this and ensure their Food and Nutrition Services Department is responsive to student needs and accountable to their Boards of Education for their budget expenditures.

With federal support and accommodations, students can take their next day's breakfast home with them every day. Also, students in some districts may benefit from healthy fruit and vegetable programs, in addition to traditional lunch and breakfast programs. This allows many students to try and enjoy fruits and vegetables that are new to them. Innovative food programs also plan Fear Factor Taste Tests to encourage students to try new healthy foods. Other food demonstrations show the consequences of less healthy food choices.

Food Services Managers may also participate with local Health and Physical Education staff to connect eating and exercise to good health and success. These efforts have led some schools to be recognized by the United States Department of Agriculture. Food service partners understand that schools are more than six hours a day, 180 days a year and they provide healthy meals and snacks for after school programs, weekend enrichment activities, and summer learning programs. Schools are one of the healthiest places where Americans are eating, and that is why districts must be actively involved with their food service operations.

- Key Takeaway: Work closely with your Food and Nutrition Services to ensure meals are both healthy and cost-effective.

COMPASSIONATE LEADERSHIP

With all the recent research and discussions about competency, change leadership, communities of learning, commitment, and collaboration, we must not ignore a leader's need for the essential ingredient: compassion. The need for compassionate leadership in our schools is more crucial now than ever before. Compassionate leaders are remarkable but do we value this trait enough? Or do we wonder if compassionate leaders have the courage to make the tough decisions when the clock is ticking? Do these leaders worry too much about people's feelings? Or are they respected because they make it easier for teachers to meet their family's needs?

Compassionate leaders reach out and treat teachers as colleagues, not as employees. They listen and offer assistance and support. They keep staff informed. They do not hide from their feelings but remain steady and in control. They lead through tragedy and stress. As our leaders feel the educational accountability crunch, they must keep the heart and soul in their schools. Anyone can create a master schedule, issue a discipline consequence, or chair a staff meeting but only those leaders who possess emotional intelligence lead with compassion.

These leaders earn respect and affirmation from their staff because of how they handle difficult, complicated situations. As districts move forward with continuous improvement initiatives and data-driven decision-making, these efforts must be successfully combined with the need for compassion in our schools. Followers will respond better to a leader who consistently displays kindness, empathy, and respect. It is not in the job description or present on the administrator's evaluation form, but leaders must be good listeners who provide understanding and support during challenging school years or when staff is experiencing personal difficulties.

How do leaders balance their need for compassion with the need for improved student learning? Researchers have found that being able to empathize, exercise self-control, and work collaboratively is a far greater measure of success than a simple IQ score. Yet, as we begin completing our principal's evaluation forms, nowhere do we see compassion or empathy measures.

Unfortunately, many employees are not often praised or positively acknowledged for their empathy. Are these traits valued? Have standardized testing and our data-driven school systems left us cold, detached individuals who simply teach to the test?

Compassion for self and others helps renew leaders and makes them more effective. A compassionate leader creates a positive place to work, and that leads to outstanding achievement and greater student success. When districts value their staff as professionals and respect them as individuals, they want to come to work and make a difference. Respecting each staff member as an individual encourages them to reach their personal goals and support school and district initiatives.

What does all this mean for leaders? Are leaders tuned in to how others feel? Do they truly care, and does the staff know it? Of course, school leaders who are only compassionate but do not value data-driven, decision-making, and standards-based curriculum, may never improve teaching and learning and not last long in their leadership post. The ideal is to be aware of the staff's emotional needs while still paying attention to the other tangible aspects of improving student achievement.

The importance of having a school leader who can balance emotions and complex data should be at the forefront of our educational improvement efforts. Do not take the heart and soul out of your day-to-day interactions in your building as you strive for educational excellence for your schools and students. For many, schools remain a welcoming place. They are a place where students and families find warmth, comfort, and discovery. Let's be sure to keep it this way.

- Key Takeaway: As school leaders, we must support our staff by showing empathy, compassion, and respect.

DISCUSSION PROMPTS

How do you support your students' emotional well-being?

What role does support staff play in your schools?

What strategies can you use to diminish exclusionary practices?

How can you ensure that all students feel connected to their school?

What strategies are in place to provide open access to high-level classes for all learners?

Chapter 4

Supporting Those Who
Need Us Most

It was a hot steamy day when this single mom and her two school-aged children were on the city street, stuffing boxes, clothes, and some favorite stuffed animals into their old, rusty car. This mom worked multiple jobs and long hours but always seemed to struggle to make ends meet. This time that struggle resulted in being evicted from their apartment and the children being uprooted once again. With both children in tears, the mom explains that this was only a temporary move and that someday they would be back in their own place.

With sweat dripping and tears in their eyes, the children arrived at their aunt's and uncle's place with all of their possessions packed in one car. Family is family, and their aunt and uncle could not turn them away, but a two-bedroom apartment at the nearby local high rise was now going to try to accommodate four children and three adults. So when the children woke up the next day to begin their walk to school, it should be no surprise that their homework was not done, their clothes somewhat disheveled, and an exhausted mom already late for work. How can we support those who need us most?

EVERYONE NEEDS AN ADVOCATE

Everyone needs an advocate, and many of us were lucky to have total support from our families. In the mid-1960s, factory jobs were plentiful in small urban communities, and getting ahead in life was still possible through hard work, with or without an advanced education. However, parents knew public education offered a chance for a better life and was the great equalizer. Although many parents were not college-educated, they wanted their children to go to college and often were not afraid to come into school and advocate for their children.

But today, children from all circumstances are left to advocate for themselves. How can we support all those students? How can we help them define their destiny? Let us be clear: American educators still believe America is the greatest nation in the world. Many are thankful every day for the public education that they received in their neighborhood public schools. Their teachers prepared them well for every challenge they would face along their educational journey.

In America, we promise a free and appropriate education to all students, and we deliver on that promise. Yet, students without advocates are left to navigate a complicated system with limited support built in. Our public schools never turn anyone away, but the American public education system unintentionally holds people back. Kids whose parents went to college—go to college. Those who didn't—don't. The best strategy to get people ahead in our nation is seriously flawed. System challenges are due to policies and procedures that have been happening for years and years. It is not malicious or intentional—but it must be fixed!

No one is a bigger public school advocate than our educational leaders and teachers. But we must be honest and take a hard look at what we are doing because even our nation's educational system is not designed to provide the same opportunities for all. It is the privileged that continue to receive the privileges. We must start supporting those students who need us most by insisting that our schools advocate for those who do not have anyone standing with them at the bus stop, school conference nights, or award ceremonies. We must insist on equity and opportunities for all our children.

- Key Takeaway: All students need advocates to support them and help them succeed.

A TRUE PROFESSIONAL LEARNING COMMUNITY

Public schools must lead the charge for achieving equity in the education sector. Districts must ensure that all students are successful, especially those students who need school support the most. Fairness is not about similar resources, culturally sensitive instruction, and open course enrollment. Making sure all students have what they need to be successful is what is fair and just. This is where discussions about equity must begin and how we can ensure success for all of our students regardless of need.

Educational leaders must develop a comprehensive support system for their students that weaves together resources gathered from the entire school community. If students do not learn, effective educators ensure that it is not due to their lack of effort, creativity, or program options. They are relentless in ensuring that students complete assignments and meet their academic requirements. This takes courageous staff members who focus on what students can achieve, set lofty goals, and encourage students to participate in demanding high school courses.

One district used its professional learning community (PLC) as a vehicle for providing this support. They provided increased student instruction time and an additional hour for teacher collaboration and data sharing. One of the most critical factors in a student's academic success is the quality of their teachers. A PLC is a forum that brings teachers together to discuss student achievement data; examine student work; use feedback from other teachers, parents, and outside service providers; analyze current research, and range in a discussion focused on professional practice and improvement initiatives.

Teachers need to work collaboratively, ensure all students are learning, design common assessments, and develop individual support plans for student success. PLCs provide the time and the setting to professionalize your school environment. Through the many PLCs held in that district, teachers continually ask themselves, "What is the goal of today's lesson? How will I know my students are learning? What will I do to ensure that they do? How will I respond to them when they don't get it?"

The teachers and administrators know that schools can and must do better. They also know that school is much more than a label or ranking on a standardized test score. They support data-driven decision-making and the creation of data teams. They understand that the most outstanding educational improvements occur when teachers get together and share their successes and failures. The solution lies in engaging learners and inspiring them. This is how public schools become more equitable and support those students who need them most.

Following are some of the ways that a community can come together to support student learning.

Rewards. Focus a PLC's efforts on student learning. The school's positive behavior support system can provide incentives to students who demonstrate academic success or supportive behaviors, such as caring about education, accepting responsibility, respecting self and others, and exhibiting positive behavior. Any staff member who observes students demonstrating these target behaviors may give the student points or the school's token economy which can be used later for incentives.

Group for extra support. Districts often use school-based mentoring programs, which means that all students meet in small groups for 20 minutes weekly for mentoring sessions. Small group instruction and additional academic support are available where and when needed. Those services

typically involve assistance and the direction of an early intervention program team. Students having difficulty in one subject area may be placed
with a subject-area teacher in a small academic support class instead of study
hall. Students may also receive help from after-school programs where they
review homework and the next day's upcoming tasks.

Students experiencing challenges in reading or mathematics can be placed
in a reading or mathematics support class run by a certified reading, mathematics, or English teacher whose direct positive approach helps build meaningful, lasting bonds with students. Double subject area blocks are also used
to accommodate students who need additional support. The goal is to provide
students with what they need to succeed without pulling them out of their
core academic subject classes.

When the number of discipline referrals and in-school suspensions
decreased in one school, the current in-school suspension staff was reassigned
to provide academic support to students. Students who miss assignments
and struggle with the school workload are scheduled into academic support
classes during their study periods, before school, or after school. Consistent
follow up and monitoring of the student is necessary to ensure that they do
not return to their old patterns.

No zeros allowed. Equitable schools do not allow a student to just opt out
of completing work. Students receive the grades they earn, but students who
do not complete assignments go to credit recovery to complete the work at
a passing level. If a student hands in an assignment on time, the student can
earn up to 100%. When a student misses a due date, the staff still insists on
work completion, and students are not let off the hook.

When the school counseling department receives information that a student
is failing, a counselor meets with the student and calls the student's parents
or guardians. The counselor then removes the student from the study hall
and off the list of approved students for early dismissal, late arrival, or any
other nonacademic time. Students may remain in credit recovery until their
teacher receives the missing work and grades the assignment at meeting
standard level.

Effective teachers. Look at who is teaching your students. Veteran teachers' experiences may be best for addressing the needs of these learners. To
provide an equitable education to all students, insist that class size and teacher
assignments reflect your goals. If that is not the case, school leaders must
change past norms and traditional mindsets and plan to reassign teachers and
readjust class sizes. Promote activities based on student interest.

The key for educational leaders is to invest time and energy in the inter-
view and selection process to ensure that they hire the best candidates for all
open positions. Having effective teachers in place year after year is essential
for eliminating achievement gaps and supporting students who need us most.

An effective teacher not only builds positive relationships with students but also supports their academic growth and development.

One student, from an economically disadvantaged background, regularly demonstrated inappropriate anger and had no apparent interest in achieving academic success. Calls to her home made no difference—there were clearly no support systems for her there. Throughout her high school career, she participated in nearly all of the school's support programs and received help with her behavior management, motivation, socialization, academics, emotional needs, and transition services.

Occasionally, she regressed, but the school saw consistent, steady progress. As we say for all students, moving forward and making progress is the key to success. She graduated, and, although no proud parents attended her graduation ceremony with a camera and a rose, the teachers and staff were there to let her know that they were proud of her. She left to go into a Job Corps program to hopefully find more success in life.

It is no longer good enough to ensure that students are taught. Teachers and administrators must ensure that all students learn. If students do not have their educational needs met despite the school's best efforts, they must not give up. Schools will need to provide additional time, support, and assistance. By giving students relevant, timely feedback, teachers and administrators can meet the needs of members of the Xbox generation, who are accustomed to instant feedback and numerous opportunities to reach their goal targets.

Students need school leaders who recognize the value of good teachers, share leadership, and are not afraid to take on challenging tasks. Students are no better than the assignments they receive, the expectations others have for them, and the support programs put in place for them. How can you ensure that all of your teachers provide students with rigorous learning tasks in environments that support them while still challenging them to be their best?

- Key Takeaway: When a student is unsuccessful, don't blame the student but look for other supports to help the student learn and succeed.

SUPPORTING ENGLISH LEARNERS

Focusing on additional English-learner support is essential if public schools are going to meet the needs of all learners. By having materials in multiple languages and consistently monitoring students' progress through formative assessments and class-generated student work, districts can ensure that their English learners advance at an appropriate pace. By providing supplementary materials and books, communities can increase a student's exposure to content and academic vocabulary aligned with the core curriculum.

Ensure that your English learners are included with their peers in academic and social settings. Not only will they benefit from the experience, but so will the other students in your school. As your English learners make growth on standardized testing measures, so, too, will your school and district recognize gains on their accountability metrics. Find appropriate venues to celebrate their successes and be sure to include parents in the celebrations. Parent outreach and engagement must be an essential component of all school goals, as it is important for our English learner's families to feel welcomed and included in our school settings.

English-learner courses should be aligned with a district's core language arts curriculum and English learner proficiency standards. Courses can emphasize oral language, academic vocabulary, and writing through thematic units and project-based learning. One essential component is that professional development sessions are provided for classroom teachers working with English learners.

Another critical factor is building connections with and engaging the multilingual families of our English learners. Some states offer the opportunity for students to receive a Seal of Biliteracy for demonstrating proficiency in English and a minimum of one other language. An award to recognize students' academic efforts and the benefits of being bilingual and biliterate is a great way to prepare your students for success in the 21st century, regardless of where they live and work.

- Key Takeaway: English learners succeed with the right support.

REDESIGNING SPECIAL EDUCATION
FOR STUDENT SUCCESS

By creating high-quality, in-district special education programs, districts can improve student services and lower costs. Facing uncertain times, increasing student need, and decreasing financial support, public school systems are searching for innovative ways to meet the needs of all learners in cost-effective student-centered environments. Redesigning the in-district special education programs can provide better learning experiences for children, improved support networks for families, and cost savings for cash-strapped districts. So how can a district provide better educational programs and garner budget savings?

The road map to success requires a four-pronged approach:

- Assure high-quality and appropriate staffing levels.

- Provide state-of-the-art facilities with the necessary equipment and learning technology.
- Create strong partnerships with community providers to support students and families.
- Insist on school support and buy-in from school leadership and staff.

As systems strive to provide a high-quality education for all of their students, keep a clear focus on meeting the needs of the large percentages of students receiving special education services in your district. With no signs of long-term financial stability or IDEA reauthorization on the horizon, districts must sustain increasing special education costs without drastically reducing educational programs for all of their students.

To complicate matters, many districts are seeing an increase in the number of students receiving free and reduced-price lunches, as there are significant increases in the number of students qualifying for special education services. For other districts, even when the total numbers of special education students have increased during the last 10 years, special education spending per pupil as a percentage of total district expenditures decreased.

In essence, special education savings can allow districts to continue to support other essential programs. Districts can save millions of dollars by offering high-quality, district-wide specialized programs in their neighborhood public schools. How can a district accomplish this result? Creative programming requires investment in high-quality and appropriate staffing and state-of-the-art facilities with the necessary equipment and learning technologies, and Board of Education and school buy-in.

It is essential to develop a district-wide continuum of services for all students to grow and succeed in district schools in their home community. The district's educational model should be based on having a continuum of services that include district-wide programs located in their neighborhood schools. Each school can be the home of one of the in-district specialized programs and be charged with leading, supporting, and enhancing one specialized program.

For example, one district elementary school can support an early intervention preschool program; another elementary school can be responsible for the program for students with autism and communication disorders; another elementary school can be the home to the transitional program for elementary students with emotional and behavioral disorders, and a fourth elementary school may run the program for students with multiple challenges and disabilities.

These programs not only control and contain direct district expenses, but they also help eliminate the need for many outplacements. Most importantly, they provide exceptional teaching staff, specialized facilities to support unique student disabilities, and a family and community partnership network. The next step should be to create middle school program options and redesign high school programming.

A unique academy can be created to be the home to students who are not experiencing success in their high school and may need a smaller, more supportive learning environment. Another programmatic cost-saving innovation can address the 18- to 21-year-old special education population. Using community space and partnerships with local providers, districts can launch programs for this student population. With these programs in place, districts will be on their way to providing high-quality programs and budget relief.

Programs for children with autism and children with communication disorders can experience outstanding success by adding sensory rooms. Sensory rooms are special classrooms designed to help autistic children and others stay calm and focus on being better prepared to learn and interact with others. Staffed by special education teachers, physical and occupational therapists, and support staff, sensory rooms have stations including light walls, bubble tubes, mirror walls, lego walls, whiteboards, bouncing balls, punching bags, ropes, climbing areas, and swings.

To ensure high-quality, cost-effective special education programs, central office leaders must prioritize them and provide consistent monitoring. Special education directors can share special education data at their regularly scheduled staff and leadership meetings. An online special education outplacement tracking tool can put real-time data at your fingertips. Central office team members and the district business directors should meet monthly with the special education team to analyze budget trends and pending placements. Use an outside agency for auditing operations as well as outplacement facilities that serve your students.

So what will you learn? When elementary-age students remain in the district, make connections to the school and greater community, are provided with a dynamic staff and innovative facilities, students flourish. Internal school-based programs can allow your students in special education to experience tremendous academic success and a better sense of belonging. As students experience success, the need for outplacements greatly diminishes, and districts benefit from the savings year after year. You can garner student, parent, staff, and community support and achieve better results by embracing a special education redesign model.

Public school is much more than achieving improved standardized test scores and increased academic indicators. School is about people—helping students and their families achieve success and reach their full potential. We all know the positive impact a caring, motivated educator can have on students. Education leaders believe in the possibility of all students and never set limits on children. Yet, we need to evaluate our special education process.

Too often, we have staff sitting through multiple Pupil Placement Team (PPT) meetings every day with overwhelmed parents who wonder if they are doing what is best for their children. Are we missing something here? Would it increase understanding and facilitate better communication if parents could discuss test results with test administrators before the PPT without school counselors and teachers listening?

Instead, we usually overfill the room with professionals, overwhelm parents, and disenfranchise participants who do not feel part of the "team." A new PPT format, which is starting to be implemented in local districts and has gained traction during the pandemic, is long overdue. A supportive structure that utilizes existing technology can be the answer. Special education case managers can email all involved the program options to be considered and ask for opinions via a formal electronic response.

Teachers complete the responses during noninstructional times. To increase efficiency, initial emails provide parents with test results, academic progress, attendance updates, and behavior reports. PPT meetings can even be held via teleconferences. In this demanding educational climate, educators must maximize a parent's visitation time. When parents come to their schools, let them observe their children in inclusive classroom settings.

This provides an opportunity for parents to see a myriad of learning strategies at work and gives them a better understanding of teaching, class requirements, and behavior intervention plans. This design demonstrates the philosophy of parents as true partners. Also, team members can provide honest responses without the pressure of a formal meeting. An email exchange eliminates the powerful influence of passionate team members. It also discourages educators from protecting "my" turf and the "not in my classroom" approaches.

Our job as educators is to keep children's dreams alive, motivate them to believe in themselves, and make sure that all students have the skills to navigate life's challenges. While we prepare students for jobs that do not exist, grit and perseverance will be critical skills for all students. As we prepare students for a changing world, public school systems should inventory school and community-based supports, and solicit new partnerships.

- Key Takeaway: Ensure special education programs put students first and look for creative solutions to return out-placed students to their home schools.

ENGAGING THE DISENFRANCHISED

A principal in a nearby district, who always focused on disenfranchised students, helped create a model program for struggling students whose needs were often not met by traditional Planning Placement Team (PPT) programming. The need to think "outside the box" grew out of his experiences and those of his colleagues whose well-intentioned PPT meetings, like the following one, were not getting at the root cause of the problems.

People exited from another PPT meeting with an upset parent, an unmotivated student, and a frustrated team. The student had a case manager, a behavior intervention plan with self-selected, specialized instruction in all core academic areas, and counseling support. Yet, with all those supports in place, the student was academically unsuccessful, clearly unmotivated, and becoming more and more disinterested in school altogether.

How could we ensure that this student did not become just another public school drop-out? Try to tailor students' high school experiences to meet their personal needs. A program composed of academic rigor, social and emotional support, and vocational training allow students to personalize their school programs. Vocational education is a good way to engage disinterested students because it gives them a choice and makes them the decision-makers in their learning. To promote interest, students should choose their jobs, design their group service-learning opportunities, and create flexible academic schedules.

Academics. Small class sizes with flexible meeting times allow students to earn graduation credits. Credits accrue monthly rather than once a year. The method used to accrue credits is the highlight of the program. Each marking period lasts 18 school days, which accounts for 10 marking periods instead of the typical four. Therefore, at the end of the marking period, students receive credit based on their performance.

Once a student earns their credit, a tenth of credit in a subject area is documented, and the student can never lose that credit. If a student fails a class, the student has the next 18-day marking period to make up that credit without penalty. Students are also supported and encouraged to take courses in the mainstream environment. The more students create their schedules, the more invested and committed they are to their success.

Social-emotional. In consultation with the program social worker and the teacher, students create individual goals for specific areas of need. Weekly and daily tracking of student behavior and emotional well being encourages student responsibility. Also, students are assessed based on their academic output rather than any inappropriate school behaviors.

Students earn privileges by accruing a certain number of points during the week, which runs Friday through Thursday. Early release time Friday is the privilege that most students work to earn and is granted only to those students who have their parents' permission to leave school early. Alternative rewards are given to those students who cannot leave early. Students also learn that there are consequences for inappropriate behavior when they do not earn the incentive.

Short-term exclusion is an in-class intervention often used to give a student a timeout to regroup and get back to class as quickly as possible. When students are sent to exclusion, they begin by sitting quietly for 10 minutes, after which they reflect on their behavior in writing and then verbally with either the social worker or the teacher. Exclusions are given for such infractions as repeated misconduct, disruptive behaviors, and intentional swearing.

Each student has a 45-minute weekly counseling appointment with the social worker. Those appointments focus on cultivating social skills, self-advocacy, emotional regulation, and behavior management. In addition to individual counseling, students participate in various student groups, such as an underclass girls' group meeting in the morning once a week. All students in the program have one organized group activity per week.

During the weekly morning meetings, members learn about issues that relate to anger management, peer relations, emotional functioning, upcoming activities, and positive weekly contributions. The group activities can also provide time for students to complete a project as a team. These activities have included cooking, arts and crafts projects, cooperative games, and activities in the community.

Participants also engage in special events that highlight notable achievements and holidays. Celebrating the positive is a benefit to students and gives them something to look forward to accomplishing. For example, students eagerly awaited the Thanksgiving Feast and began asking about it in September. They collaboratively divide the tasks, create menus, make invitations, shop for groceries, decorate the dining area, and prepare menu items. The climax of the Thanksgiving Feast was when the students welcomed school staff to their school site and served a tasty meal that they prepared from scratch.

Although it is beneficial to host such events, it is even better to hold events celebrating the students' successes. The school community celebrates students' birthdays and behavioral achievements and when students add mainstream classes to their schedules, make honor rolls, and graduate from the program or the school. Celebrating the success of their peers motivates students in the program and helps create a supportive, caring, and compassionate learning environment for all learners.

Monthly off-site field trips were added to the schedule as well. On the second Tuesday of the month, students and staff members participated in a field trip to such places as ropes courses, restaurants, museums, farms, and amusement facilities. When staff members create the field trip schedule, they ask for input from the students, who enthusiastically share their ideas. Students are even more excited when they visit places that they have suggested. Students, who had never gone or been welcomed on field trips before, joined appropriately and had a great time.

Decades ago, the US Department of Labor supported vocational training as a key schooling option for students and families. The report stated that mastering vocational skills would help students gain competitive employment and earn a decent living. Thirty years later, there is a renewed interest in vocational training, especially from students.

Each student works with the program's vocational educator to determine appropriate placement. This may mean that the student is placed at a school-secured job site. Students may also be placed at a neighborhood convalescent home, the town grocery store, a local child care facility, a district elementary school, or numerous fast-food restaurants. Students may also find their own employment options. Either way, the vocational educator monitors the placement and awards academic credit based on the number of hours the student works and the quality of their work. Students earn elective credits every year for completing this work component successfully.

In addition to work-study opportunities, the program includes service-learning experiences such as making biweekly trips to a local soup kitchen, reading at the local elementary schools, playing games at the nursing home, or creating a flower garden to improve the appearance of their high school. To get students excited about the gardening project, they visited a flower show and met with a horticulturist. Students saw flowers they liked and wanted to include in their garden. Participating in the planning process increased their investment in the project.

Each month on "Coffee House Friday" students prepare baked goods and beverages to serve to staff members who come to the pseudo cafe. The music department provides music while the cafe is open. This project teaches students about the hospitality industry and increases interaction between students and staff members from the larger school community. Positive relationships with staff members from outside the program makes students transition to mainstream classes and co-curricular activities much smoother, helping them experience success and build their confidence and school comfort level.

AVOIDING THE SUMMER SLIDE

Educational leaders are always concerned about a lack of learning over the summer months. Do not let the summer slide negatively impact all of your improvement efforts. Summer learning opportunities can provide all students with enrichment activities, acceleration, and learning recovery. Students need to be able to read proficiently if they are going to experience school success. Start your reading intervention in the early grades and provide student choice at their appropriate level so all students can develop a love of reading.

So what can we do? Consider student transition years and create programs that expose them to their school, staff, and curriculum. Create summer learning adventures and summer school programs that combine high-interest reading selections and engaging digital content with physical activity. Create personal reading targets for all students. Ensure that small daily group instruction with appropriate instructional level text is part of your learning program.

Students can benefit from reading preselected adventure book sets based on their Lexile levels. Let students take ownership by setting their own Lexile goals, graphing their progress, and journaling about their reading. Students need to be able to personalize and take charge of their learning. Capture students' immediate attention by selecting engaging illustrated books. Recognize student progress along their journey so you can promote a love of reading with your students. Comprehension strategies can benefit all students and will require regular practice and consistent monitoring.

Design personalized reading pathways and collaborative work for all your learners. Together, they can create visual presentations that focus on the main idea, characters, and story details. Allow students to share their learning and reading with their classmates through hands-on, fun, and engaging tasks. Create summer learning with a culminating event. Join the superintendent for a book reading that features the book on a big screen, a raffle for students, and, most importantly, a strong message to encourage reading.

Provide students with bags filled with grade leveled books to take home for more summer reading. Books should be the ones that will be featured in their classrooms next school year. This initiative is a low-cost way to encourage reading at home. Building a love of reading and seeing how happy and excited students are to receive bags of books is a reason enough to launch your summer program. Regular attendance and academic support can give students a jump start in the new school year. Do not let another summer slide by—start your program now.

Districts may also consider offering summer STEM Enrichment opportunities. While traditionally an in-person learning experience, the pandemic provided an opportunity for districts to provide exciting summer virtual camps. The STEM Camps can occur over the summer, whether in person or at a distance, and include fun and engaging activities involving science, technology, engineering, and math. This summer, many students joined camp facilitators online in a Google Meet for approximately 30 minutes twice daily. All materials were shipped directly to their homes to ensure a safe, productive learning experience.

Districts can develop Summer School Camps for middle school students. These programs incorporate educational experiences in collaborative games, fitness and nutrition activities, and current event exercises. One morning per week, middle school students could attend local nonprofit camps to continue learning, participate in group activities, and have fun. Districts may consider holding these programs at one of the high schools to have better access to the pool, kitchens, and other facilities and to get students accustomed to and excited about high school.

Many middle schoolers welcome the opportunity to have something to do in the summer as it provides them a chance to make friends and try out new activities. Some families cannot take elaborate summer learning vacations or send their children away to costly overnight camps at expensive college campuses, but all families can take advantage of a free district-provided program. School systems must step in and ensure these types of experiences exist and are fun, not simply another traditional "summer school" program.

Some districts implement Summer Bridge programs for students transitioning between Grades 8 and 9. This program works with rising at-risk ninth graders during the preceding summer with follow-up during the school year. The Summer Bridge program provides entering ninth graders a jump start to high school, and much needed support for identified at-risk students. The program includes academic, career, social/emotional, and character development components taught by high school teachers and counselors.

Typically, the program runs for three weeks in the summer and includes a Ninth Grade Seminar for half a credit so that students can start ninth grade with some banked credits. The program engages students in various learning experiences with expeditions to nearby state and private colleges, visits to ropes courses for team building, local businesses, and excursions to other places of interest.

The program's final day showcases students' displays and celebrates their work for their parents, administrators, and community members. Students who participate in the program receive high school credit and their high school-issued device. During the following school year, they receive ongoing support from transition counselors to ensure they pass their courses, are "on track" to be promoted to tenth grade, and understand the importance of B's or better.

In many districts, high school students are allowed to keep their devices over the summer and, therefore, have the opportunity to take online courses taught by in-house teachers for credit. Courses can include various topics such as Financial Literacy, Introduction to Psychology, Art, Drawing, and many others. Credit recovery courses are also often offered online during the summer at the high school level. Usually, the online curriculum has been aligned to the district's classes, and students have the opportunity to make up partial or full credit during the summer.

Districts can look for opportunities to partner with various nonprofit organizations to provide additional summer programs. Often, local agencies that support the children's health, development, and early learning in the district's home community can partner with schools to provide free summer programming for students. These programs may focus on summer reading and field trips to fun learning places and events that help expand students' horizons, cultural awareness, and social skills.

Districts should seek out partnerships with other agencies to offer grant-funded programs to their students. These grant-funded programs can help facilitate students from urban and suburban districts across the state to come together to participate in summer enrichment programs. This is where they learn how to interact with each other in a natural setting that encourages diversity and inclusion.

- Key Takeaway: Create excitement around reading and launch creative summer learning programs, so another summer does not slide away.

COMMUNITY LEARNING OPPORTUNITIES

The GEAR UP Program (Gaining Early Awareness and Readiness for Undergraduate Programs) provides a combination of federal funds and state higher education institution support to public school systems. Some state colleges and universities are awarded a federally funded grant, GEAR UP, from the United States Department of Education. By partnering with local community colleges and public school systems, this program makes a difference for public school students. Students and families use grant services to see how college can be a real option.

GEAR UP supports student success and promotes college and career readiness to increase the number of students who graduate from our public high schools and enroll in college. All eighth grade students in partnership districts are eligible to receive services funded by the grant. Most importantly, GEAR UP services move with eighth graders through high school and their first year of college. High school services include college visits, intensive support, and advising with college and financial aid applications, and a scholarship opportunity.

Additional GEAR UP programs include PSAT Test Bootcamps with MasteryPrep; Tutoring/Academic Support; STEM Enrichment and Exposure; Mentoring; and College Knowledge Workshops/ College Advising and Information about financial aid for college. Additionally, eighth graders can participate in the Math Depot. The Math Depot is an after-school program that helps students gain mathematical mastery and readiness for ninth grade and beyond. Students not only have the opportunity to build their overall confidence and critical thinking skills, but they are also mastering additional school challenges in a supportive environment.

Local YMCAs and other not-for-profits can be active supporters of all district initiatives and work closely with disengaged and disenfranchised youth. As providers of after school and enrichment programs, these agencies offer many opportunities for job shadowing, internships, and job placements. High schools may also host Child Care School Readiness Preschool Programs in their schools. These fully operating licensed daycare centers and preschools are exploratory classrooms for high school students interested in pursuing careers in education. These classrooms also help support district efforts to recruit and diversify their staff.

- Key Takeaway: Students need opportunities to interact with community providers and their staff.

DON'T FORGET YOUR STAFF

When we are looking to improve ourselves, we look for a coach to support us. Do we value coaching enough in public education to include these positions in our budgets? We embrace coaching with athletes, but what about educators? Progressive school districts have created a culture of coaching in their schools that is supportive and compassionate. How can we support those who need our help the most?

Teachers want students to do well. Personalized learning has been one vehicle that has positively impacted students' learning. Let your most successful teachers design professional learning models that can be implemented through a coaching model. These coaches work closely with teachers, and resources are focused on increasing student achievement.

There is not just one way to be a successful coach or only one style of coaching. Respect, trust, and a student-centered focus are the keys to successful coaching relationships. Let your coaches be non-evaluative. Make sure they understand that students can adapt to any learning environment. Lastly, if they are also knowledgeable about curriculum expectations, your teachers will appreciate and thank them even more for the support.

Coaches need high emotional intelligence to focus on the positives, have empathy, and not expect perfection. Coaches must learn from their mistakes, not be afraid to fail, and possess a growth mindset. The best coaches are hard-working, self-motivated, and masters of their craft. Coaches must have an area of expertise and the ability to build confidential, trusting relationships.

Coaches need clarity around job objectives, model options, and measurement criteria. Coaches need to be good listeners, nonjudgemental guides, and transformers of teachers' practices. Coaches must be lifelong learners who continually perfect their craft but always go out of their way to share the best teaching strategies. Job embedded professional learning provides all teachers with an opportunity to pilot new strategies in their public school classrooms.

Coaches must develop teachers so those teachers can enhance student learning. The best coaches do that by respecting staff, providing timely and specific feedback, modeling effective instruction, and monitoring teacher growth. Coaches need to be aware of data collection, data analysis, and data usage if they are to engage in high level instructional discussions with staff. By maximizing people's potential and ensuring continuous growth, coaches will create a continuous improvement system that will benefit all educational stakeholders, especially students.

Consider a peer-to-peer coaching strategy as most teachers welcome additional instructional support from their colleagues. Great teachers are continuous learners who are always searching for ways to meet the needs of their students more effectively. Collaborate with your teachers' union to ensure that coaches are supported and valued. You can strengthen teaching and learning across your district by empowering coaches and giving them the authority to lead. Great coaches have always allowed players to learn from their mistakes and to celebrate successes. Teachers need to see their own areas of success, challenges, and opportunities.

Coaches provide examples of specific strategies in practice and document the student's role in the learning and evidence of student mastery. Coaches can gather and analyze data from online programs and then share in an easy-to-use format with teachers. Online programs target specific learning gaps that require improvement and assist teachers in maximizing core instructional time. Just as our students learn in multiple ways and through different modalities, so do our teachers. Coaches recognize the uniqueness of their teachers and students.

By asking probing questions, soliciting feedback and input from teachers, and encouraging self-reflection—coaches guide learning, not just provide answers. Successful coaches are present in teachers' classrooms to interact with students, view classroom routines, monitor curriculum implementation, and support rigorous instruction. Building administrators become stronger instructional leaders when they work closely with instructional coaches and embrace coaching models in their schools.

School teams can position themselves for individual student growth, whole class progress, and overall school success by meeting regularly to collect, review, and analyze individual student and whole class data. Help school leaders better understand the curriculum and create a school-wide culture of collaboration by involving them in regular meetings that focus on individual student data.

5 STEPS TO CREATING A CULTURE OF COACHING

- Eliminate teacher isolation
- Insist on a growth mindset
- Clarify coaching responsibilities
- Determine what success looks like
- Leave the evaluation process to others

Public schools cannot operate in isolation! Teachers welcome the support and appreciate having someone with expertise in their field to bounce off their ideas. By creating a culture of collaboration and embedding coaching into their improvement efforts, public schools will give teachers what they need to ensure that all students are successful, especially those who need us the most.

- Key Takeaway: Educators welcome the support of coaches as long as they are collaborators, not evaluators.

DISCUSSION PROMPTS

How do you support students who are struggling academically or feel disenfranchised?

What mechanisms are in place for teachers to discuss student performance data?

How have you creatively met the needs of students requiring special education services?

Who are advocates and mentors in your school?

What strategies are in place to ensure learning occurs over the summer months?

Chapter 5

Challenging All Learners

What an exciting year! We had two eighth grade middle school students receive perfect scores on the Smarter Balanced Assessment. Never before have we had a pair of students like Bryce and Xavier. Both were involved students with supportive families, and both had incredible academics. The high schools were already preparing for their nationally recognized semifinalists. The high school principal greeted Bryce's mom with "Congratulations! I can't wait to have your son at our school."

The high school was fresh off a $100 million renovation. This mom knew the system well as she was a teacher in the district. The high school principal was beaming, but the parent looked ashamed, almost embarrassed, from all the positive attention. When the principal asked if everything was alright, the parent barely could get out the words, "I'm sorry, but Bryce will be attending a private high school as he and his friend, Xavier, have committed to Kennedy Academy."

ELIMINATING BARRIERS TO ACCESS

Who will be the next top performer? The only way school districts will know is to eliminate barriers to access. The best way to ensure access is to collapse academic levels; eliminate tracking at their schools; adopt no-zero grading practices; open access to advanced placement and all high-level courses; provide SAT preparation workshops; eliminate course prerequisites; go one-to-one with devices, and place community college satellite branches in their high schools. High performers and most motivated learners will appreciate having equal access to a high-quality education program that prepares them for success in college and life.

K-12 public school graduates will be truly ready for college success and beyond when public schools increase academic rigor for all and remove any school and policy barriers to high-level coursework. Encourage your students to continue to improve their SAT scores. Students should be scheduled to take advanced placement courses in their areas of interest and strength. These strategies will enhance students' college admission opportunities and ensure that we challenge all of our learners.

Our nation's best colleges and universities are looking for well-rounded students with unique talents and advanced skill sets. These skill sets must be more than high SAT scores, pristine high school transcripts, and rigorous course loads. Supporting students as they write their college essays is essential. This is an opportunity for students to tell their family's story. Essays should showcase the student's determination and strength to attend college, as many of our public school graduates are still first-generation college students.

Public schools that want to ensure college and career success provide rigorous academic programs, career exploration opportunities, life skills, and activities for independent thinking. Most importantly, these schools change mindsets. They ensure that all their team members do not set limits on children. As the great equalizer, public schools show they care about students by challenging them to attain the skills and training they need to compete in the competitive global world that awaits them. Provide opportunities for your students to problem solve, collaborate, debate, design, and create. Have we accounted for all the jobs lost to machines and new careers made by technological advances?

Reading, math, problem-solving skills, attendance, school anxiety, and social comfort are factors that determine the probability of students attending college. Solid academic skills are no longer a guarantee of future success. Focus on creating a balance between academic strengths and emotional stability. To prepare students to attend college and experience success once there, we must teach our students the importance of perseverance and why grit matters.

K-12 public education and higher education will positively impact our nation's economy and our society's growth when they value student engagement, recognize the variety and individual traits of all learners, and allow students to design and create. Public schools can set the stage for substantial student growth by embracing digital tools, creating student-centered classrooms, scheduling with personalization, and designing learning environments where all students feel comfortable and respected. Colleges want students with unique, varied skill sets and a track record of school and community involvement.

- Key Takeaway: High schools have to open up their curricula to include more engaging student practices and allow students to take responsibility for their learning.

KEEPING THE ARTS ALIVE

Some school districts have doubled their district's commitment to the arts even with limited funding and accountability systems. These districts knew schools had to be more than just academics. They also knew that the district needed one person responsible for coordinating the curriculum, launching events, providing leadership, and embracing innovation. Districts tap current teachers, reduce the teaching load, and pay a modest stipend. For once, the arts can hit the home run.

For the concept to work, the right person for the job needs to be tapped. There needs to be someone who knows the district, who knows the students, a teacher leader who has taught music or art, appreciates both, and has a firm belief that the arts could help the district meet its academic and climate goals. The perfect candidate can inspire, motivate, and challenge students and staff alike. The coordinator also should consider creating a district-wide data team for elementary music and visual arts. Too often, music and art teachers work in isolation in their buildings and have very few opportunities to learn from each other.

Your coordinator also should modernize the arts programs with digital resources and ensure that all elementary schools receive music software. The entire district should be provided with a software program that offers a digital assessment, parent communication, instrument inventory, music cataloging, and fiscal management system. Fine Arts departments can focus on digital presentation tools, digital portfolio design, tablet use, and digital gallery presentations. Having a clear continuum of services ensures that music and art have a place in all K-12 programs.

Many of your students' creations should adorn your school's hallways as well as public spaces such as the public library, City Hall, and Board of Education meeting room. Encourage all of your middle schools to schedule students for both music and art. This assures that all students are exposed to both arts and are immersed in the core elements of the national core arts standards: Create, Perform, Present, Respond. Unique offerings like ceramics, digital animation, guitar, piano, and world percussion can give students voice and choice in their learning.

To expose high school students to as many visual arts and music classes as possible, all visual arts classes and many music classes can run as semester courses for half of the school year. Instrumental and choral ensembles should run full-year courses and meet daily. Students appreciate having a choice in their learning and the option of taking medium-specific classes in their interest area.

As districts face numerous budget challenges and competing interests, consider forming partnerships with youth theaters, local art galleries, and senior centers. Collaborative partnerships are vital to assuring that the arts survive any budget crisis. By providing music and art teachers a greater voice and supporting their work, public schools can achieve positive increases in academics as well as climate and culture indicators. While the positive signs of progress cannot be solely attributed to the increased focus on the arts, districts see the advantages of more students participating in arts programs.

Be proud that your schools are more than just core academics. Secondary schools should feature a full complement of athletic teams and high-quality music programs that highlight choral and instrumental instruction. School musical and drama productions feature students on the stage, in the pit, behind-the-scenes, supporting event organization, and show marketing. Arts in the Park showcases student artwork and musical performances at your local park for the community to enjoy! Districts often display student work in Gallery Walkthroughs at their high school foyers. These experiences cannot be replicated in traditional classrooms.

- Key Takeaway: The days of only academics are over; appreciation of the arts is paramount for a well-rounded education.

THE ACTION OF ATHLETICS

While making her daily commute to work, the principal would see Hector jogging to school. Well, it was more of a sprint. A quick beep and a friendly wave were the daily morning routine. After school, when making her rounds, the principal would see Hector in the gymnasium weight room. A quick hello and a friendly wave were the daily afternoon routine. Hector was a member of the cross country team, indoor track team, and outdoor track team. Hector had only been in the district since eighth grade when his parents moved to Connecticut after two years in Arizona and a lifetime in Mexico.

After four years of running for the high school teams, Hector was prepared for his big day. It was the State Finals and an extremely important day for Hector since it could mean scholarship opportunities and his ticket to a better life. Hector already would be the first person in his family to graduate high school. Now he was one race away, one victory away, from realizing his dream of attending college.

School systems committed to the full development of their students realize that high-quality athletic programs, like music and art, are essential components of the high-quality public school experience. By offering a full array of competitive sports teams for boys and girls, school systems create a healthy way to extend the school day and create a vehicle to teach the valuable lessons of commitment, teamwork, effort, and success.

While fitness needs to start in elementary school, competitive sports teams should begin in middle school. Let student interest drive your sports programs, just like your elective course offerings. Based on student interest, one district recently added a middle school swim team and a lacrosse program. While fitness and wellness are an underlying benefit of all sports programs, the most significant benefit is knowing your students are involved in healthy, well-supervised learning experiences after school hours.

To encourage participation in school-based athletic programs, districts are providing summer sports clinics for younger children. These clinics are run by high school coaches and are one small, inexpensive way to increase student participation in sports. When students reach high school, they can be incentivized to play sports through creative personalized learning programs that offer credit for their participation. Students can earn elective or physical education credit for meeting state standards through active involvement in their school athletic teams.

In addition to all the student-athletes, competitive sports programs allow students to serve as managers, statisticians, game announcers, event filmers, and activity organizers. These programs involve hundreds of students, and many other students attend school contests as spectators. We know that the more time educators have with their students on school grounds, the better the school spirit will be, and the more tremendous positive respect students will have for each other and the entire school community.

- Key Takeaway: Athletics today involves much more than playing a sport; it promotes leadership, teamwork, and respect.

ENRICHMENT OPPORTUNITIES ACROSS LEVELS

As charter, magnet, and private schools offer enrichment opportunities and a promise to challenge even the highest performers, it has become essential that public schools provide enrichment opportunities that challenge their students as well. Elementary schools should provide before- and after-school partnership programs for skill development, student enrichment, and learning acceleration.

These enrichment opportunities should be provided for students who demonstrate the skill level and the desire to participate in an innovative year-long program after school and on Saturdays. All elementary schools should feature competitive Math League teams and a Field Day event for their students. In one district, elementary students in third, fourth, and fifth grades are selected to participate in a district-wide Saturday Enrichment Academy which offers academic enrichment programs in mathematics and science. Program selection is based on student achievement data, student commitment, and attendance.

The program's goal is to provide activities in math and science that are in addition to the curriculum being taught in the classroom. The components of the course include an online classroom environment as well as in-person-based activities used in developing 21st century skills. Saturday enrichment academics, after-school STEM clubs, broadcast clubs, and numerous clubs that provide volunteer opportunities have generated student interest and are well received by students, staff, and families.

Another district reallocated textbook funding, created innovation labs for middle school students who need a challenge, and offered after-school STEM Academies. Students complete design thinking projects that incorporate writing code for project creation on 3D printers. They study robotics and launch rockets using engineering principles. Their culminating activity is flying a drone. Students also coded CNC machines to explore engraving and routing of wood and metal products. The program provides a challenging after-school learning experience where like-minded students work together to enhance their STEM skills.

Students welcome the opportunity to have STEM Academies in their schools. Be proud to offer all students programs that challenge them, inspire them, and support them. Parents and students appreciate these opportunities, and it is truly an honor for students to be selected for these programs. These programs add additional quality learning experiences and help foster a love for math and science with elementary and middle school students. We hope this passion carries over to high school, where there are opportunities to take advanced science, technology, engineering, and math courses.

- Key Takeaway: Saturday and after-school programs motivate students to explore new avenues and are welcomed by both students and families.

STUDENT-DESIGNED PERSONALIZED LEARNING

Having exhausted all core and elective science course offerings in high school, Sarah, a college-bound senior, searched for more learning opportunities in the sciences. Sarah planned to work in the science field someday, so she wanted to pursue advanced studies in STEM courses. She knew she needed advanced knowledge and experiential learning in high school science work. Sarah met with a Personalized Learning Experience (PLE) Coordinator to design an academic plan that would provide her with the science exposure she was looking for in high school.

Sarah is one of the hundreds of students in our district taking advantage of credit-bearing opportunities to create a program, develop a talent, or explore a career option while embracing anytime, anywhere learning. The PLE is a necessary addition to the high school core classes due to limited in-school offerings and jam-packed student schedules. This experience provides students with greater choice, voice, and flexibility in their learning and college preparedness.

Students are held accountable for skill attainment and mastery of content. Learning objectives tied to standards are a key component of the PLE application and must be met before receiving credit. School counselors and faculty sponsors review PLE proposals with the high school students. Our district creatively worked with the teacher's union to utilize the teacher duty period to support PLE staffing.

Both our high schools had a diverse group of teachers who volunteered to become PLE coordinators. Teachers utilize their duty period to assist students with PLE design, solicit community and business partnerships, and navigate the PLE application and approval process. PLE coordinators have two periods daily to support students. Students with an approved PLE must maintain a log of their learning targets and validate when objectives are met.

Students also share culminating projects that demonstrate that the learning standards have been achieved and student learning documented. Learning target applications require PLE description, PLE expected outcomes, criteria for successful PLE completion, anticipated hours of the PLE, reasons for selecting the PLE, key components of the PLE, and location(s) where the PLE learning experience will occur. Students earn high school credit through authentic, real-world learning experiences at our schools, local businesses, and community agencies. Participation is on the rise, and PLEs are here to stay.

Students who design PLEs find the learning experience very valuable. Two high school students, Charlotte and Mia, directed a play as their credit-earning PLE. Charlotte was hooked on the play because she felt her classmates would relate to the topic and enjoy it. While they had trepidation about performing the play, they felt its message was meaningful for all. Ava designed a PLE related to special education as she thought she could be helpful and make a difference. Her project involved working with students during gym class. Ava is now considering a career working with children with special needs.

A "We Build" on-site PLE learning experience with contractors was created when both high schools underwent extensive renovations. Matias, who participated in the "We Build" program, recommends personalized learning experiences to others because learning goes beyond the classroom. He

MERIDEN PUBLIC SCHOOLS
Here, Students Succeed

PERSONALIZED LEARNING EXPERIENCE (PLE)
APPLICATION

Please complete both pages of this form with the PLE Coordinator and Faculty Sponsor. The PLE Coordinator is available to assist the student in developing the PLE Learning Targets. All information must be complete before beginning PLE in order to earn credit.

Student Name: _____   Date: _____

Faculty Sponsor: _____   Student ID Number: _____

Timeframe: (S1, S2, Y1) _____   During Period: _____   Grade Level: _____

PLE Title: _____   Requested Credit: _____

Subject Area/ Department: _____   Grading Method: (Letter or P/F) _____

Student should obtain the first four signatures & return completed form to the PLE Coordinator.

Student: _____   Date: _____

Parent: _____   Date: _____

Faculty Sponsor: _____   Date: _____

School Counselor: _____   Date: _____

PLE Coordinator: _____   Date: _____

Principal: _____   Date: _____

Routing	PLE Coordinator	PowerSchool Manager	School Counselor	PLE Coordinator
Please initial & Date				
	form completed & recorded	section created & schedule revised	PLE reflects graduation plan	Records management

Figure 5.1a.

welcomed the opportunity to work with skilled tradesmen and tradeswomen. Another student participating in the PLE program decided to explore career options in engineering and architecture. PLEs are different from the core academic subjects because they combine specialized topics with real-world experiences.

PERSONALIZED LEARNING EXPERIENCE (PLE)
LEARNING TARGETS

PLE Description/Summary:
Describe expected outcome(s)/standards-based learning objective(s) of this PLE: (attach applicable standards - CCSS and/or content specific)
Criteria for successful completion of the PLE, including assessments:
Anticipated hours for successful completion:
Reasons for selecting this PLE: Explain why you are pursuing a PLE and what you hope to learn from the experience.
Document the components of the PLE and the learning environment/location where the PLE will take place:
Other information to be considered:

Figure 5.1b.

One high schooler, who had enjoyed the personal finance course she took as a sophomore, created a PLE that allowed her to work alongside a teller at the local credit union branch. Her PLE taught her about confidentiality, professional attire, and acceptable work behavior. Other students explored areas of interest ranging from providing technical support at a district courthouse and mastering Python programming. Some innovative projects included creating games for students, trout preservation projects with the local river watershed authority, and working with a local hotel to improve their environment and sustainability efforts.

Personalized learning experiences have provided the opportunity for many high school students to earn high school credit. The program's success can

MERIDEN PUBLIC SCHOOLS
Here, Students Succeed

PERSONALIZED LEARNING EXPERIENCE
GUIDELINES FOR SUCCESS

➤ Students will meet with school counseling staff and faculty sponsor to review the PLE proposal.

➤ Students will maintain a PLE log and develop a culminating project to demonstrate that learning standards have been successfully met.

➤ A high school student may earn up to two full *academic* credits in any school year through the Personalized Learning Experience program.

➤ Students will have a minimum of five (5) scheduled credits in addition to their PLE credits.

➤ PLE credits will count towards elective graduation requirements if successfully completed.

Figure 5.1c. Personalized Learning Experience Application. Meriden Public Schools, Meriden, CT

be determined by listening to your students and by the improved academic and climate and culture data. PLEs have become so popular with students that middle school students are beginning to discuss PLE ideas. Students look forward to having flexibility in their course schedules to create their own self-designed personalized learning experiences. Redefine teaching and learning in your pursuit of true student-centered learning environments.

The following essential questions will help guide your efforts. What is the role and function of the high school counseling department? What is the purpose of high school study halls? What methods are in place to allow middle school students to earn high school credits? What is the district's relationship with the local Chamber of Commerce and the business community? Are you allowing all level students to keep school-issued personal technology devices over the summer? Does your staff support more personalized learning? Do you provide summer learning opportunities for academic and social-emotional growth?

Share how students can learn anywhere and anytime by highlighting your personalized learning experience program. We know school needs to be more than just academics. Encourage your students to take charge of their learning by implementing a PLE program in your district. This will allow you to personalize learning, provide students with a voice, and improve engagement in technology-rich environments.

Broaden and deepen your understanding of the different pathways students take toward developing the skills and knowledge needed for college and career success. Districts can purchase "real world" industry connection platforms that allow industry professionals to engage with classrooms through virtual visits, industry chats, and recorded sessions. These programs alert students to greater choices in their careers.

- Key Takeaway: Students welcome opportunities to connect student learning to career experiences.

PORTRAIT OF A GRADUATE

Many districts have created or are in the process of developing their Portrait of a Graduate, which describes what a high school graduate needs to know and be able to do to be successful in life. This usually takes the form of a visual representation that shows the traits and specific indicators that a graduate should have upon graduating. Representations include about four to six attributes, with specific indicators developed for each attribute. Inherent in the Portrait is the theme of equitable opportunities and advocacy for all learners.

Portraits may be designed in various ways, depending on the district's interest, uniqueness, and creativity. These visuals are then prominently displayed on district and school websites, t-shirts, banners, flyers, posters, and mailers to gain support for their district. Another purpose that visuals serve is to ensure that all stakeholders are aware of the Portrait and that it becomes a natural extension of the school system's image.

Often, districts include a Portrait of a Graduate as part of a larger vision for the district's Strategic Plan or District Improvement Plan. More important than the graphic, however, is the process. Most districts can devote anywhere from two to five years developing their Portrait, which is completed

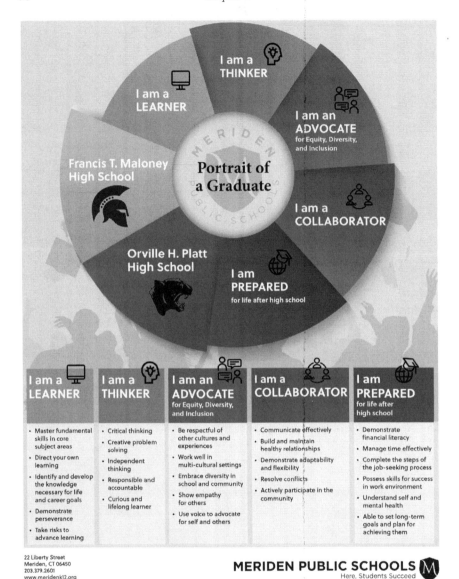

Figure 5.2. Portrait of a Graduate. Meriden Public Schools, Meriden, CT

in multiple phases. Rather than adopting a top-down process, districts try to incorporate diverse perspectives from a wide range of stakeholders, including the school community and external community members.

In the first phase of the work, and depending on the district's size, a Working Team may be established consisting of representatives from central office, building administration, teachers, counselors, supervisors, parents, students, union representatives, board members, and community providers. This team meets regularly to ensure broad participation from all key stakeholders. The voice of the community must help drive the school systems' goals for their graduates.

Depending on the individual district, key stakeholders may include student groups, teacher groups, local business leaders, graduate alumni, college administrators, religious groups, trade union representatives, sports coaches, community providers, city government officials, police, and community-based youth groups. Input from these groups can take the form of structured interviews, focus groups, virtual meetings, community meetings, and online questionnaires and surveys.

Each district approaches gathering input unique to its own needs; the only constant for any community-driven portrait of a graduate is that the public's voice is heard loud and clear in their public schools. One district may conduct 10 focus groups; another may need to conduct hundreds of focus groups. Public school systems vary significantly in size, but all serve students and families with a free appropriate public education. Once the Portrait of a Graduate is developed, then the next phase begins with a broad range of priorities, depending on whether the Portrait is part of the district's or community's larger plan.

Priorities may include, but are not limited, to action plans for dissemination of the Portrait across schools and community, engaging stakeholders in conversations about the Portrait's purpose and attributes, creation of teacher instructional groups to assess whether the instruction is aligned to the competencies, development of a data framework for measuring Portrait competencies, or expansion of curriculum and programs to close gaps in opportunities to attain Portrait competencies. Public schools remain the best place to provide all students with the skills and attributes they need to live happy, healthy, and successful lives.

- Key Takeaway: Involve all stakeholders in creating your district's vision of a Portrait of a Graduate for the 21st Century.

BUILDING A COLLEGE AND CAREER CULTURE

If we are going to challenge our highest performers, we need to expand college visit opportunities, realizing that many students lack the resources, support, and ability to visit independently. Many of our students are the first in their families to be thinking about going to college. For some students, these visits will be the first time they have ever ventured onto a college campus.

Recognizing this, we must greatly expand college visit opportunities; ninth graders can visit an in-state college campus, and tenth graders can visit local colleges. In contrast, eleventh and twelfth graders can visit four-year and two-year colleges of their choice. Virtual college tours using virtual reality may also help broaden horizons for students whose families may not have the finances to travel out of state for a college visit.

Schools should provide career exploration activities along with the importance of high school coursework and transcript seminars to all incoming ninth graders. School staff should participate in one-to-one conferences with students to discuss student attendance, student participation, student academic progress, and student satisfaction with school. Continue these one-to-one conferences in the tenth, eleventh, and twelfth grades as well.

Get students and families to start thinking about career goals, SAT scores, rigorous course selection, and the importance of achieving B's or better by offering ninth grade homework clubs and family dinners. In addition to tenth graders visiting colleges, they should also tour potential worksites and begin their pre/post-college exploration activities with the help of school mentors. Small and individual college and career planning meetings should take place with eleventh grade students and their families.

The importance of Spring SATs should be shared with students and families. As more and more colleges diversify their admission criteria, schools should continue to rethink how best to use their time and resources. In the senior year, weekly college readiness and career preparation seminars should be held with all students. High schools' College for All Campaigns should include college awareness activities, assistance with the college application process, and college visitations.

Ask The Expert Programs encourage high school students to meet with teachers who have graduated from a college the student is interested in attending. The teacher shares their college experience and answers college questions. Alumni Seminars allow students to interact with recent alumni and learn about the college experience directly from someone in school. Often, graduates can provide relevant information that is not found in the college descriptions and catalogs.

Public high schools must assist students with their college application process by offering College Application Boot Camps where the staff helps students create their Common Application account. School staff should also provide seminars, FAFSA Workshops, and Military and Apprenticeship Roundtables to support the varied interests of their students. Recruiters representing each military branch can coordinate the Military Roundtables for students to meet and learn about a military career. Students need to know about the military's requirements, benefits, training schedules, and timelines to make the most informed decisions.

Have you Completed your
FAF$A?
Free Application for Federal Student Aid

On average it only takes 23 minutes to complete online

No matter what path you choose after graduation, completing the FAFSA will open doors for education and training. Check out the link below to access free resources to help you with your FAFSA completion!

https://bit.ly/MPSFAFSANOW

Figure 5.3a.

FAFSA
State
Priority
Deadline is
February 15

Maloney
High School
121 Gravel St
Meriden, CT 06450

Platt
High School
220 Coe Ave
Meriden, CT 06451

Here, Students Succeed

Figure 5.3b. FAFSA. Meriden Public Schools, Meriden, CT

Apprentice training coordinators from local unions can meet with students to share all the available opportunities in the trades. Students interested in the trades need to know what an apprenticeship is and how they might participate in one. These connections with local business people and tradespeople can open up new career options for your students. College Application Campaigns (#WhyApply, #I Applied, #Accepted) generate excitement and motivate students to attend college. Scholarship Fairs provide information and eligibility criteria to help students and families decide which college makes the most sense for their families.

College and Career Readiness tools, parent and student communication tools, Twitter, and advisory classes can be used to share information with your students and families about scholarship opportunities. Let the culminating activity be Senior Signing Day. Use the auditorium, a big screen, and have students walk across the stage with their college, military branch, or the company of employment logo prominently displayed. Let your most popular teacher be the master of ceremonies and invite the junior class to be in the audience. This is an opportunity to celebrate and show community stakeholders the power of public education.

Your students' satisfaction and fulfillment with their careers will define true school success. All students can and should be encouraged to enroll in Advanced Placement (AP) course offerings now that there are no barriers to access high-level learning or challenging courses. While PSAT benchmark data is a strong indicator of academic success, we know that this alone should not be the sole indicator for whom is scheduled and seated in Advanced Placement courses.

One district uses PSAT scores, course grades, courses taken, and student surveys to create its own pool of potential AP students. When meeting with students and families, use these multiple data sources to encourage and support enrollment in advanced placement offerings. Assure students and families that additional support is available for all students enrolling in an AP course.

That may not be enough for some, so one district superintendent sent personal letters to the students and families who had been identified as candidates for AP course enrollment. That letter was followed up by having the school counseling department reach out to the student and family. Sometimes, it may take a little more effort and convincing to ensure that students challenge themselves with college-level coursework.

AP Boot Camp, held before the school year begins, provides students with strategies and time management skills to succeed in AP and ECE courses. Tutoring is available in-person for students, and some districts contract for online tutoring, which may have 24/7 support. Consider having your

Board of Education pay for SAT testing and provide all 11th graders an SAT Preparation course.

Additionally, many districts start early, allowing eighth graders to earn high school credits in subjects typically taught in high schools like Algebra 1, Integrated Physical Science, Spanish 1, and Modern Fiction and Poetry. These credits provide students with room in their high school schedule to earn college credits. Explore innovative partnerships with your local community college. Perhaps, in exchange for the free space in your schools, they will provide tuition-free seats for your students.

We have seen how vocational learning experiences have engaged disenfranchised students but we also hear from the business community that high-quality school-based vocational programs benefit students, businesses, and the economy. Prepare your students with technical and employability skills that they can use in the real world by offering certification-bearing vocational programs. Many high schools recognize vocational-technical schools as a great partner for their students, offering manufacturing, culinary arts, and other courses which may be unavailable at their traditional public high schools.

Our progressive public school district partnered with their vocational-technical public school system to offer their students an after-school program that provided their students with the trade skills and credentials to leave school ready for competitive employment. For our school district, it started with one young woman with a dream of being a professional chef and owning her own restaurant someday.

When her school counselor met with her to discuss her career inventory survey, it became clear that this student's passion was cooking and food service. However, there was one small problem—her school did not have a food lab to offer culinary classes. This is where innovation and partnerships came into play. The district partnered with the vocational-technical school, and this young woman participated in a comprehensive culinary after-school program. This is how public schools must work individually with their students to keep their dreams alive.

In the real world, people negotiate, mediate, articulate, argue, manufacture, experiment, plan, reflect, design, build, teach, play, relate, anticipate, and create—all without a safety net. They are on their own. We must stop having our school day consist of highly controlled, artificially contrived teacher-directed activities because it does not work for our most disengaged and disenfranchised students, as well as many other students. The more developmentally appropriate we can create our school environments, the better it will be for all learners.

Work opportunities and volunteerism outside the school are motivators and incentives for students. Many of the least academically motivated students are the best workers and volunteers. A quality vocational component program ensures that all students have exposure to the real world workplace, lifelong learning options, and personal growth and health considerations. Those competencies, not another standardized test score, will enable students to contribute to the betterment of society successfully.

Build your alternative programs with a solid foundation of academics, social and emotional support, and vocational training. Yes, success is achievable because students are partners in creating their learning programs, and you can bet those programs will have a well-designed vocational focus. By focusing efforts on real-life experiences, necessary work skills, and respect for oneself in one another, educators can help students enjoy success in school work and life.

- Key Takeaway: Start early, hold high expectations for all students, and provide innovative and rigorous college and career readiness opportunities.

DISCUSSION PROMPTS

How do you encourage students to participate in extra and co-curricular learning activities?

What college credit-earning options do you have available for your high school students?

How do you support students and families with the college process?

How can you acknowledge and honor your senior graduates?

How can you assure that your students are prepared for success after graduation?

Chapter 6

Celebrating Success

Her mom and dad were educators, her dad retired after teaching high school math for 35 years, and her mom was in year 37 as a successful elementary school principal. Her mom had just announced her retirement to an adoring staff. Yet, their daughter, Cindy, struggled in her second year of teaching after enjoying over a decade of success in the business world. Cindy is a sixth grade English Language Arts teacher at a middle school. Her students' test scores were low, classroom referrals high, and student engagement and effort were not where they needed to be for success.

After another tough day, Cindy visited her school's principal. She had enough and was ready to quit, throw in the towel, and just give up. The principal reminded her that teaching was her passion and long-term goal. At the same time, they both agreed that things needed to change. Giving up was not the answer. Cindy worked on classroom management, utilized digital content, created a more student-centered classroom, and visited peers getting exceptional results with their students.

Now four years later, Cindy is one of the district's highest-performing teachers, ranking in the top 10 percent for student growth gains and her school's nominee for the district's Teacher of the Year. Her success can be attributed to her relentless effort, willingness to accept support, and unwavering commitment to her students. These are the types of results we must celebrate and share with others.

WHY IT MATTERS

We must not walk away! We must stay in our roles. We must fight for high-quality education for all. Despite budget challenges, increases in poverty, homelessness, housing instability, and students lost and searching for purpose; we must protect public education in America. Will we be committed to hearing the voices of our students and supporting them in changing American public education for all? It's been done in some districts, and now we can do it across this great nation. Stop and listen. Transform your school system and offer hope to all students by insisting on respect.

Why be so passionate about this? Because we have all witnessed how districts can be reinvigorated, turned around, and students' lives positively impacted forever. Today in America, without education or vocational training, career opportunities are few and far between. We must change this, especially for those who need us most. Many parents want more for their children but they do not know how to help.

Too often, there are no SAT prep classes, no college visits, no college planning counselors, and certainly no privileged college admissions. Many families rely solely on public schools for college and career support. And again, the inequities continue. What programs can we implement to ensure that all public school students are prepared for college, career, and life success?

How can school counselors with large caseloads possibly support all of their students alone? What about all the students who do not have supportive parents? Or those who do not have a roof over their head? Those who struggle with their own mental health issues? Those who worry about where is their next meal? Who will ensure it matters for them? Who will provide the necessary support?

We must redesign American public education to create a system that ensures all students have equitable access to educational opportunities in systems where partnerships are nurtured, technology leveraged, the whole child embraced, equity advanced, students challenged and supported, and success celebrated. Only then will public education receive the respect it deserves and our students the education they were promised. This is how we will ensure that all students have a chance for a better life.

- Key Takeaway: We all must work together to ensure our American public education supports all learners.

STUDENTS AT THE CENTER

Creating an authentic, judgment-free environment that welcomes transparency, embraces collaboration, and ensures success regardless of background must be our mission. This philosophy insists that there is zero judgment and that all decisions revolve around the well-being of the students. All decisions have a domino effect; when one piece shifts, it impacts the sequence of events that follow. Despite changes in the community context, students, staff, and

Figure 6.1a.

Figure 6.1b. Road Map to Student-Centered Learning. Meriden Public Schools, Meriden, CT

district, the goal should be to create an accepting and supportive learning environment for all students.

As violence and poverty increase in the community and school populations shift, decisions need to be made to support achievement and rigorous learning for all students. All decisions made by the central office team and the unions must collectively support three reflective questions: why do this, how do we do it, and will it improve the lives of our students? When teachers understand why a change is occurring and how collectively we can improve, we will create an inclusive environment where students flourish, and staff feels supported.

Remain open and honest regarding the importance of what is happening around you and the impact your consistent systems and structures can have on your success. This structure must revolve around your student and staff success, be revised based on data and teacher input, and continue to evolve with your ever-changing demographic. This structure owns what we as a community can control while acknowledging that there will always be factors we cannot influence.

Always remain transparent with your stakeholders, staff, students, and families. This practice will remove the sense of failure from all, support consistent reflective practices, and encourage structural change. Overall, your sense of resilience will remain strong if you have developed operations, systems, and structures to survive inevitable change. These protocols and formats will foster a sense of trust among students, staff, and families. The hope must be that these effective practices remain strong beyond the superintendent's tenure so that the district and community will continue to thrive despite undeniable challenges.

Develop leadership at the school level and empower principals and teachers to be creative and innovative in their practices. With the support of your unions, create instructional leadership teams with the staff in each of your schools. This will lead to shared strategies and increased opportunities for student growth. The process will ensure that ideas are put into action based on the needs of all students across all schools and all grade levels.

Organized transparency and shared leadership structures help districts create reflective and action-based mindsets. Work with your teachers to ensure they are supported and held accountable while encouraging best practices. Ensure that your staff is consistently tasked with presenting innovative ideas and offered school leadership roles. Teachers must maximize instructional minutes every day. Align small group instruction, differentiate student learning, and perfect instructional delivery across schools and grade levels.

District and school-based leadership teams must reflect on areas of improvement and collectively determine subsequent academic and instructional initiatives based on what students need. While we do not know what lies ahead, your vision must remain the same: all students will learn without judgment. By focusing on individual student needs and analyzing student progress regularly, districts will guide teaching and learning with transparent and accurate data.

STANDARD TESTING IS NOT THE ENEMY

Success means positive student results. Standardized testing can be used as a motivator when not viewed as a threat or teacher evaluation tool. Problems arise when districts misuse these scores. Our enemy is not standardized testing. Standardized testing has a place in your continuous improvement efforts. Do not be derailed by parents wanting to exempt their children, communities feeling targeted, and elite private school communities abandoning standardized tests together.

Some public school critics and anti-testing groups will share that every child is an individual, and societal challenges impact results, and most public school advocates agree. Other critics will question the amount of time dedicated to testing, and most public school advocates would agree. However, we must insist that all children attend schools where they are challenged and supported. This is why schools must have mechanisms in place to track student growth and improvement every year.

Standardized testing provides educators with the following information:

- English Language Arts and Math performance by student, class, and school
- Individual student goals and performance targets
- Areas for focus with instructional coaches
- Teachers whose students are making growth gains

Respect teachers who inspire children to think, discover, and achieve their dreams and wishes, as these are the instructors who continue to see improved standardized testing results for their students. Many districts honor teachers with significant growth gains with recognition ceremonies at Board of Education meetings, district-wide celebrations, and back-to-school convocation events.

Honor, support, and cherish your teachers. Ensure that they have standards-based curriculum, instructional pacing guidelines, common formative student assessments, and ongoing professional development. Our students need to be prepared for an increasingly complex society. Empower teachers! Teachers should be the decision-makers when it comes to granting students more time, additional practice work, demanding rigorous assignments, or creating opportunities for more student voice and choice in their learning. Effective teachers strike an effective balance between engaging classroom instruction and good performance on standardized testing.

Develop excellent relationships with union leaders and your staff. This partnership can lead to private foundation funding and grant opportunities. Ensure that all stakeholders understand, appreciate, and value student growth as a key success indicator. Public school stakeholders should ask themselves two simple questions: Is what we are doing working for all students? How do we know it? Matched student growth scores are a good indicator of how well your district is performing.

Your teachers can embrace the challenges of standardized testing if you let them lead the charge. Teachers want their students to be happy and successful but they also want great results. Most teachers will not stop until they achieve success. All significant performance indicators will improve when there is a healthy balance between giving students voice and choice in their learning and expectations are consistently held high for all students.

Respect your great teachers and recognize them for their hard work. Support these teachers, help them be innovative, and encourage them to put students at the center of all learning. Create schools where students and staff feel supported, and use standardized testing to help launch your improvement process. By focusing on continuous growth and setting clear, tangible goal targets, students and staff can work together to achieve success.

- Key Takeaway: Use standardized testing to support continual growth and improvement in teaching and learning.

LEADERSHIP LEVERS

Your path to success requires dedication, discipline, and a desire to continue to make yourself and your team better. Your staff, like your students, are very different. While some staff is highly motivated, easily inspired, and committed to continuous growth, others may become complacent and content. For them, good might be "good enough." So how will you use your leadership levers to move your diverse team from good to even better?

Determine your leadership levers and your areas of strength before implementing your strategy for moving your team, your schools, and your students to greater success. Most district leadership teams are made up of numerous administrators with diverse backgrounds, unique talents, and a vast array of leadership levers. This core group of eight leadership levers or inspirational traits can be essential to your district's growth and success.

While not all members have all of these traits or can pull every lever to their advantage, all members possess a few leadership levers that can be utilized when situations present themselves. Compassion and empathy, content and curriculum, charisma and influence, climate and culture, community connections, creative and cost-effective, candor and calm, and curiosity and challenge are some levers we have seen influential leaders utilize to navigate situations successfully for their students and stakeholders.

There is not just one path to greater success. Each of us must create our own personal roadmap to improve performance and better outcomes. By identifying the real you, selecting your leadership levers, valuing and celebrating the uniqueness of yourself and your team members, you will create a system that is committed to continuous improvement, values growth, and celebrates greater success.

Once your team recognizes and understands your leadership levers, they can reflect on where their strengths lie, respect the leadership levers of other team members, and start to work on those levers which can contribute to their personal growth, thus supporting the overall success of your students, schools, and district. In addition to understanding your leadership levers, new board members and administrators can also benefit from understanding the political and financial context and constraints that public schools must navigate regularly.

It is just as important that your school board is both knowledgeable and supportive, and that requires training. Training for new board members and administrators typically includes professional development in leadership, budget management, policy review, effective teaching (curriculum, instruction, and assessment), and parent partnership. To be successful, today's orientation programs must include discussing the importance of demanding respect, building support, and celebrating success.

This can only be achieved if district's challenges and students' needs are acknowledged, and teachers and students are supported. We need inspired teachers who encourage our children to dream and to believe. By promoting a positive culture through rewarding experiences, boards and administrators can keep teachers focused on district goals, initiatives, and student learning. If we are going to redesign American public education, we must listen to our students. We asked them what they would do to "fix" their school?

And this is what they told us. Don't set limits, challenge me, support me, believe in me, and stop taking the devices away from us. As leaders, we need to change the mindsets of educators, value growth and effort, and celebrate achievement. If the work is important enough for us to assign, we must find creative ways to get our students to complete it. Students are just asking for an opportunity to be seen as unique individuals. Change your systems and structures to put students at the center.

- Key Takeaway: A strong, diverse leadership team contributes to the collective growth of your district.

LEADERSHIP THAT INSPIRES

Facing intense pressure for continuous improvement, value-added growth scores, and improved teacher evaluations, we must not ignore the importance of our leaders' ability to inspire their teachers. As we create attractive schools and learning institutions that students, staff, and families want to attend, the need for inspirational leadership in our schools has become most apparent. Keep your citizens and educational leaders inspired, committed, and driven to improve student achievement.

But how can you maintain this focus? How do public schools continue to inspire their students and teachers when the public demands more with less available resources and greater responsibility? How do you motivate yourself when mandated assessment methods do not provide you with the data you need to show success? It is up to the inspirational leader to find ways that will effectively convince stakeholders that the positive results are worth the work.

It is not always necessary to utilize prepared words, or a pregame pep talk to inspire a team. We know that prepared remarks and canned speeches are not always effective motivational strategies. Sometimes it just takes being honest and transparent. The true test of any leader is how you respond during the most challenging times. You need to keep focused, maintain your composure, and encourage the team to believe that they can. Motivating the team to work hard and want more requires leaders to support and genuinely care about their team leaders. You must anticipate problems and provide proactive interventions.

Inspirational leaders know when to pull back or push strongly ahead. Be aware of staff overload and always provide fair and honest feedback. Exhibit humility, tenacity, and grace, even during the most challenging times. Remain prepared, articulate, and determined. Maintain your emotional intelligence in all exchanges with students, staff, and stakeholders. You can make a big difference by simply offering a personal thank you or a small token of appreciation.

Your staff needs to know they are valued and respected. When leaders put the global needs of schools or organizations before their personal needs, desires, and wishes, they create a loyal staff. Listening and empathizing are two key traits that inspirational leaders exhibit when working with their staff. They recognize the uniqueness of their team and personalize their motivational strategies.

By being accessible, trustworthy, and approachable, even when the tension levels are at an all-time high, you will gain greater respect and authentic buy-in from your team. Keep your focus, maintain your composure, and encourage your team to believe. Anticipate the problem, proactively respond to the issues, and be compassionate. By supporting and caring about their employees, inspirational leaders build positive connections and motivate their teams to work hard and want more.

The word inspire makes us think of a positive force, a motivational presence. However, can you inspire someone through the use of their shortcomings? Can one be inspirational if they lead with fear or are unrealistically demanding? As we examine the effectiveness of using supportive, constructive feedback over destructive criticism when motivating others, we offer a few real-life situations that represent exchanges that commonly occur between leaders and those they influence.

It was the city's annual football banquet and any youth football player would have been thrilled to be invited. This eighth-grade student was honored to attend and the invitation softened the blow of a tough loss in his football team's season finale. He felt excitement and anxiousness as he met the local coaching legend, his future high school coach. He thought how lucky he was to meet his high school coach before any of his classmates. He wondered what the coach would ask him.

Coach approached him. "Tough loss, huh?" He was thrilled for this moment. "Yes, but I should have played better." The cranky veteran coach said in a demeaning manner, "I am sure that would have helped. Now, go home, eat more, get bigger and stronger, and I will see you when school starts." The coach proceeded to walk away. The young man was mortified and fighting back the tears. His excitement and enthusiasm were destroyed.

Another young man, who was not as athletically inclined, recalls playing Little League baseball. One hot afternoon, as his team played against the league's best-ranked team, he joined his teammates as they began chanting at the opposing pitcher, "We want a pitcher, not a belly itcher!" His coach gently rested his hand on the boy's shoulder and asked, "Do you think the pitcher's nervous?"

The boy shrugged his shoulders sheepishly and replied: "I do." The coach added, "I know I would be nervous out there. The whole team is counting on him to throw strikes, and he's on the mound by himself. That's a lot of pressure for anyone!" He then pointed to the batter and said, "I am sure he is nervous as well. Do you think he would be more comfortable and at ease if we cheered him on?" The boy again shrugged his shoulders as the coach said, "Let's try a positive cheer."

The coach called a timeout so he could talk with his batter. As the coach returned to the team bench, he heard the boy leading the team loudly in cheering words of encouragement. The batter's look of nervousness and tension turned into determination and courage. While this boy never heard what the coach said to the batter during that timeout, he heard a more important message that day. That message was to work hard, do your best, and always be positive.

Many years later, this young man completed his first college assignment: a 13-page composition. He could not wait to receive feedback from his well-respected professor. He took his time, did the research, and, unlike in his high school years; he put in the level of effort reflective of his academic abilities. He was proud of himself. Two weeks later, the professor was very complimentary as he discussed the overall performance of the class.

The young man's excitement level was at an all-time high when, all of a sudden, as the professor passed his desk on one of his walks up and down the student aisles, he stopped mid-sentence and threw a rolled-up pile of papers onto the young man's desk saying, "This is unacceptable work!" The young man was horrified, deflated, and angered all in a single moment. The professor had been carrying around this young man's paper during the entire class with the calculated plan to embarrass and make an example of one of his newest students. It was not long before this student's enthusiasm for this class was diminished along with his drive to succeed.

These scenarios demonstrate the importance of inspirational leadership. The Little League coach was an inspirational leader that promoted respect, support, and encouragement. Each situation invokes in us a series of emotions that can be used to influence change. However, with an inspirational leader, some of these situations nurture and inspire a drive to continue, a hunger for accomplishment, and the motivation to achieve a goal. Let your life experiences help develop your leadership styles and affirm your operating principles.

Anyone who has been publicly embarrassed will likely avoid the situation that generated those feelings. Today's educational environments require encouragement at all levels—students, staff, and stakeholders. Our schools are learning environments where everyone needs to be and deserves to be respected. A supportive climate will encourage students to take risks and acquire new skills. Students need the ability to innovate, imagine, and inspire. We understand that today's students will need these skills in the future to be effective, inspirational leaders and advocates for change.

Districts want to encourage an understanding of the urgency that we do not lose sight of public education's value, importance, and success. When we ask students, parents, administrators, and teachers themselves what qualities and skills they expect their teachers to possess, we tend to get the same responses. They want our educational professionals to be intelligent, caring, dedicated, respectful, and indeed inspiring.

Board members and superintendents must ask if they can inspire by focusing only on a team member's shortcomings. Can we motivate ourselves if we lead with fear or are unrealistically demanding? Supportive, constructive feedback is much more effective than destructive criticism. We are in a time when we need to accept that in American education, factors like poverty are not excuses. These realities can present themselves in urban, rural, and suburban districts across our nation. The formula to support students living in crime-ridden neighborhoods must include real support and inspiration.

Schools in high-poverty areas need more teachers and resources to close the gap between those students whose birth gave them a head start and those whose birth did not. Educational and governmental leaders must decrease criticism and competition while being inspirational, supportive, and collaborative. This formula works with individual student achievement and can also work with overall educational reform.

- Key Takeaway: Student success in graduating from high school, college, and being career ready often depends on a supportive and collaborative culture.

CONTINUOUS IMPROVEMENT FOR SUCCESS

Like any successful organization, school systems must embrace an innovative and progressive continuous improvement system founded on collaboration and staff development. This system not only will guide a district's work, but it is how team members embrace these initiatives, implement them with fidelity, and believe in each other and their students that matter most.

Many districts create District and School Improvement Plans, which identify and organize improvement priorities, connect student achievement to adult behaviors, creatively support district and school initiatives, increase class rigor, and promote higher student expectations. When student success is linked to teacher accountability and support, districts have realized the greatest academic gains.

Teacher/Administrator Dashboards, utilized by many districts, display teacher/administrator attendance, classroom discipline referrals, and student assessment data. These personalized dashboards use the same gauges used to evaluate students' academic performance, attendance, and behavior. Using a growth model, you can calculate individual student growth over time, comparing standardized data by class, grade, school, district, and state averages. Use these data points to provide support and professional development for your staff.

There is a great deal of vital work to be done across every district in every town in America. If we are to succeed, our dedicated and inspired teachers will lead the improvement efforts and guide our students through their hardships. Yet, we are demoralizing our teachers with unfair criticisms and impossible expectations. How can we expect this practice to do anything but make our teachers unmotivated and uninspired? How can we expect to entice the best and the brightest to become teachers if we keep minimizing the profession?

The teacher is the number one in-school factor for student success! However, out-of-school factors like poverty, hunger, homelessness, community instability, lack of positive role models, parental pressures, and disengagement are critical factors in a student's academic and emotional success. We need to stop scapegoating public education for all of our society's failures. Public school students continue to learn, graduate, and go to the best colleges and universities in the world.

Just as we have celebrated our students, we must do the same for our teachers and staff. Classroom walkthroughs and attendance at school events are opportunities for our leaders to show appreciation and support the work of our educators. Teachers also appreciate being recognized for honors such as a grant award, leadership project, or recognition by a community organization.

A simple note or a brief email can go a long way to let your teachers know they are valued and respected. Also, treat your teachers as true professionals and provide opportunities for them to participate in professional learning opportunities of their choice in the comfort of their own homes on professional development days. These gestures of appreciation go a long way to creating a positive work climate that we know makes a difference in student content and learning.

Some districts have implemented more formal ways of recognizing teachers and staff. Teacher of the Year Receptions, Exemplary Achievement Project Awards, and providing Leadership Academies are ways districts can highlight teachers. Our district has each school select a building Teacher of the Year. This person is then recognized at a school breakfast and awarded a coveted parking space for the upcoming school year.

The school awardee then participates in the selection process for the district Teacher of the Year. A District Teacher of the Year, chosen by a committee of administrators and union representatives, is announced at a district-wide Teacher of the Year reception. Family members and colleagues are invited to celebrate with all Teacher of the Year candidates. Each teacher is presented with a plaque during the ceremony by the Superintendent of Schools and Teacher and Administrator Union Presidents.

The District Teacher of the Year is announced at the celebration, and there is always a standing ovation. The District Teacher of the Year and Building Teachers of the Year are honored at the Back-to-School Convocation, attended by the entire district. The District Teacher of the Year also inspires colleagues when sharing opening welcome back remarks. In addition, the district teacher's name is engraved on a plaque that hangs in a prominent place in the boardroom.

Another district encourages teachers to participate in its Exemplary Achievement Project Award program. Teachers submit their most creative projects to a committee of administrators and teachers, which selects the top projects to be exhibited in the boardroom at a reception. Teachers then can view these projects and replicate the ones they would like to try in their own classrooms.

You may also partner with your teachers and their union on awards programs for students. Our district's teacher's union initiated a highly successful program, Project Excel. This program honors the top 10 seniors from each high school at a special dinner to which the students and their families are invited. These students recognize their most influential teachers, and their names are included in the student biographies published in the event brochure. Nothing is more rewarding for a teacher than to receive thanks, praise, and appreciation from their former students! Ticket sales and ads help defray the cost of the event.

Also, launch recognition programs based on student progress and growth. Teachers can be recognized as star performers when their students outperform district, state, and national norms on standardized testing measures. Our school district honors teacher SBA star performers with a framed certificate of accomplishment and an actual blue ribbon to place proudly on their classroom walls. Students and visitors have a regular visual reminder of class successes. Some teachers have received yearly awards for their students' performance gains, and their classroom walls have multiple years of success.

Look to recognize those teachers who are leading the change efforts. Do not waste the opportunity to learn from them and share their strategies for motivating students to perform at the highest levels of success. One teacher shared how she used the district-provided SBA target award cards. This teacher got students excited about reaching their individualized goals and earning incentives like earbuds, LED flashlights, ice cream, tickets to home

Figure 6.2a.

games or school musicals, and other student-selected rewards provided by the district. Everyone wants to feel valued, appreciated, and respected. How will you make your teachers know they matter?

Let us look at individual student growth, have students compete against themselves, and praise teachers for any such successes. Standardized testing should be about self-improvement, and the teachers and schools should be judged on how well they help students make personal gains. American

Figure 6.2b. Project Excel Award. Meriden Public Schools, Meriden, CT

public schools should be proud! There is no lottery, no weeding out, and no exclusionary practices. Public schools take every child in a community and give those children a formal education and the opportunity for a better life.

In the end, we will not improve our nation's public education system by blaming the teachers, the parents, or the school leadership. We will strengthen our public schools by supporting them and creating cultures and climates that

Figure 6.3. SBAC Target Award. Meriden Public Schools, Meriden, CT

Figure 6.4a.

Figure 6.4b. SBAC Winning School Award. Meriden Public Schools, Meriden, CT

inspire students and staff, foster collaboration among all stakeholders, and get people excited about achieving a shared vision and national goals. We need to start promoting cooperation through encouragement, motivation, and inspirational leadership.

- Key Takeaway: Remember to praise your teachers for the outstanding work they are doing in their classrooms.

DISCUSSION PROMPTS

How do you recognize and acknowledge student and staff success?

How can standardized testing support continuous improvement and student growth?

What can you do to support and inspire your staff?

What are the key leadership traits of your most successful team members?

How do you ensure that your students, staff, and families receive the respect they deserve?

Congratulations

is a MPS Scholar!

Your average on SBAC tests for
English Language Arts and Mathematics
places you in the State of Connecticut's
highest performance category.

We are proud of you and encourage
you to continue to do your best!

Sincerely,

Mark D. Benigni, Ed.D.
Superintendent

Here, Students Succeed

Figure 6.5a.

MERIDEN PUBLIC SCHOOLS M

Congratulations

is a MPS Scholar!

Your average on the SBAC test for
English Language Arts

places you in the State of Connecticut's
highest performance category.

We are proud of you and encourage
you to continue to do your best!

Sincerely,

Mark D. Benigni, Ed.D.
Superintendent

Here, Students Succeed

Figure 6.5b.

Congratulations

is a MPS Scholar!

Your average on the SBAC test for
Mathematics

places you in the State of Connecticut's
highest performance category.

We are proud of you and encourage
you to continue to do your best!

Sincerely,

Mark D. Benigni, Ed.D.
Superintendent

Here, Students Succeed

Figure 6.5c. MPS Scholar Meriden Public Schools, Meriden, CT

IN CLOSING

American public education remains the most inclusive, effective educational system in the world. While there is still much to learn from the successes of other nations' innovative educational initiatives, America must continue to insist that its educational system is not defined by PISA Test scores or other international ranking measures, but rather by its ability to continue to be the great equalizer for so many children and families.

About the Authors

Mark D. Benigni, EdD, is the award-winning superintendent of the Meriden Public Schools, the school system from which he graduated and his own children attend. Dr. Benigni is recognized as a transformative leader who is leading his district to its highest achievement scores through collaboration and innovation.

Barbara A. Haeffner, assistant superintendent for teaching and innovation, is known for leading digital transformation and creating student-centered learning environments where student voice and choice truly matter.

Lois B. Lehman, the coordinator of grants and special programs and a curriculum expert, garners philanthropy and foundation support to create equitable learning environments that challenge and personalize learning for all students.